Tony Buzan

Tony Buzan is the originator of Mind Maps®,
Founder of The Brain Trust and the Brain Cl[
Mental Literacy®.

Born in London in 1942, Tony Buzan graduated from the University of British Columbia in 1964, achieving Double Honours in Psychology, English, Mathematics and General Sciences. In 1966 he worked for the *Daily Telegraph* in Fleet Street, and edited the *International Journal of MENSA* (the high *IQ* Society).

As one of the world's leading authors, he has published 44 books (42 on the brain, creativity learning and Mind Sports and two volumes of poetry). His books, which include *The Mind Map Book: Radiant Thinking, Use Your Head, Use Your Memory, Make the Most of Your Mind, Buzan's Book of Genius* and *Study Guides – The Next Generation* have now been published in 50 countries and translated into 22 languages. His classic BBC book *Use Your Head* has sold over a million worldwide.

Tony Buzan has become an international media star, featuring in, presenting and co-producing many satellite broadcasts, television, video and radio programmes, both national and international, including the record-breaking *Use Your Head* series (BBC TV), the *Open Mind* series (ITV), *The Enchanted Loom* (a feature-length documentary on the brain), and numerous talk shows. His two latest videos are *MindPower*, distributed by BBC Video, which teaches Mind Mapping techniques for business use, and which won a top award at the 1991 IVCA Festival, and *If at First ...*, a new way of looking at how to transform failure into success.

He advises governments and multinational organizations (including BP, Barclays International, Digital Equipment Corporation, Electronic Data Systems, Hewlett Packard and IBM), and regularly lectures to leading international businesses, universities and schools. Among members of the Young Presidents' Organization (the YPO, an international organization of multimillionaires) he has become affectionately known as 'Mr Brain'. He is Founder of the Memoriad (the World Memory Championships) and Co-Founder of the Mind Sports Olympiad (the 'Mental Olympic Games'). Much of his work is devoted to helping those with learning disabilities. He is also the holder of the world's highest 'creativity IQ'.

In the early 1990s Tony Buzan launched two major initiatives: first, the Academy, which provides extended courses and seminars on Mental Literacy, Business Intelligence, artistic and cultural intelligence, all taught in the context of *mens sana in corpore sano* ('a healthy mind in a healthy body'); second, the Intelligence Institute, which provides a hundred of the world's finest brains as an intellectual task force to assist corporations, governments, foundations and educational institutions in charting their way through the intellectual challenges of the twenty-first century.

Tony Buzan is an adviser to international Olympic coaches and athletes and to the British Olympic Rowing Squad as well as the British Olympic Chess Squads. He is an elected member of the International Council of Psychologists and a Fellow of the Institute of Training and Development. He is a Member of the Institute of Directors, a Freeman of the City of London, and is also a Patron of the Young Entrepreneurs' Societies of both Cambridge and Bristol Universities. Adding to his list of honours, including the YPO Leadership Award, was his recent recognition by Electronic Data Systems (EDS) with the 'Eagle Catcher' Award – given to those who attempt the impossible and achieve it!

ALSO BY TONY BUZAN

Books
Use Your Head
Use Your Memory
The Mind Map Book: Radiant Thinking (with Barry Buzan)
Master Your Memory
Memory Visions (workbook for *Master Your Memory*)
The Brain User's Guide
Make the Most of Your Mind
  Harnessing the ParaBrain (Business version of *Make the Most of Your Mind*)
Buzan's Book of Genius (with Raymond Keene OBE)
Get Ahead (with Lana Israel)
Brain Sell (with Richard Israel)
Man v Machine (with Raymond Keene OBE)
Spore One (Poetry – Limited edition)
Study Guides – The Next Generation (25 vols)

Videotapes
Use Your Head
The Enchanted Loom
Buzan Business Training
Family Genius Training
MindPower
If at First ...
Get Ahead
Learning with Lana

Audiotapes
Learning and Memory
The Intelligence Revolution
Make the Most of Your Mind
Supercreativity and Mind Mapping
Buzan on the Brain
Buzan on Memory
Buzan on Reading
Buzan on Radiant Thinking and Creativity
Buzan on Success
Buzan on Body and Mind
Genius Formula
Brain Sell

Other Products
The Universal Personal Organiser
'Body and Soul' (Master Mind Map Poster)
The Mind Map Kit
Master Your Memory Matrix (SEM) 0-10,000
The Use Your Head Club Manifesto
The Use Your Head Club Magazine
Mind Maps Plus

THE
SPEED
READING
BOOK

Tony Buzan

BBC BOOKS

To my dear, dear Mum, who so lovingly and so
caringly introduced me to the beauty and power
of the word; the beauty of power of the *mind.*

External Editor-in-Chief, Vanda North

Published by BBC Books
an imprint of BBC Worldwide Publishing
BBC Worldwide Limited, Woodlands
80 Wood Lane, London W12 OTT

First published in 1971 by Sphere Books Limited
Revised and updated 1977 by David & Charles
Revised and updated 1988
Revisded and updated 1989
This revised edition published in 1997
Reprinted 1999

ISBN 0-563-38312-7

Mind Map® is registered trademark of the Buzan Organization 1990
Mental Literacy® is a registered trademark of the Buzan Organization 1994
Radiant Thinking® is a registered trademark of the Buzan Organization 1994

Designed by Gwyn Lewis
Illustrations by Alan Burton, except for Plate III © 1997 Magic Eye Inc.

Printed and bound by Martins the Printers Ltd., Berwick-upon-Tweed
Colour separations by Radstock Reproductions Ltd, Midsomer Norton
Colour printed by Lawrence Allen Ltd, Weston-super-Mare
Cover printed by Belmont Press, Northampton

Contents

Editor's Foreword   7

Author's Foreword   8

Appreciation   9

Introduction   How to Use *The Speed Reading Book*   10

Division One – Exploring Your Speeds   14

Opening Quiz   14

Chapter 1   Where Are You Now? Check Your Normal Reading
Speed and Comprehension   16
Self Test 1 The Intelligence War – At the Front with
Brain Training   17

Chapter 2   The History of Speed Reading   27

Chapter 3   Reading – A New Definition   33

Division Two – Your Amazing Eyes   36

Chapter 4   Gaining Control of Your Eye Movements to Increase
Your Speed and Comprehension   36
Self Test 2 Art – Primitive to Christian   46

Chapter 5   Eye-Deal External and Internal Environmental Speed
Reading Conditions   53

Chapter 6   Guiding the Eyes – A New Speed and Range Reading
Technique   58
Self Test 3 Animal Intelligence   62

Chapter 7   Onward to Super-Speed Reading – The Speed Reading
Hall of Fame   69

Chapter 8   Meta-Guiding Towards 'Photographic Memory'
Reading Levels   79
Self Test 4 Are We Alone in the Universe? Extra-
Terrestrial Intelligences   89

Chapter 9   Developing Your Advanced Skimming and Scanning
Skills   97

Chapter 10 Your Relativistic Brain – Multiplying Your Speed by the
New Metronome Training Method   103
Self Test 5 Baby Brain   105

Division Three – Super-Concentration and Comprehension *112*

Chapter 11 The Common Reading Problems – Sub-Vocalization, Finger-Pointing, Regression and Back-Skipping *112*

Chapter 12 Improving Your Concentration and Increasing Your Comprehension *120*

Division Four – Developing Your Advanced Speed Reading Skills *125*

Chapter 13 Mind Mapping® – A New Dimension in Thinking and Note-Taking *125*

Chapter 14 Using Knowledge of Paragraph Structure to Increase Speed and Comprehension *130*

Chapter 15 Previewing – Your Mental Reconnaissance *132*

Chapter 16 Developing Your Mastermind Vocabulary (I) *Prefixes* *134*

Chapter 17 Developing Your Mastermind Vocabulary (II) *Suffixes* *142*

Chapter 18 Developing Your Mastermind Vocabulary (III) *Roots* *147*

Division Five – Becoming a Master Reader: Advanced Use of Your Eye/Brain Systems *153*

Chapter 19 The Mind Map Organic Study Technique (MMOST) *154*
Self Test 6 The Awakening Earth: Our Next Evolutionary Leap – The Global Brain *156*

Chapter 20 Getting Control of Your Newspapers, Magazines and Computer Screens *164*

Chapter 21 Creating Your Knowledge File – Your Brain's External Data Bank *171*

Chapter 22 Getting Full Value from Literature and Poetry *173*

Chapter 23 What You Have Accomplished So Far – Your Extraordinary Possibilities for the Future *179*
Self Test 7 Your Brain – The Enchanted Loom *179*

Self Test Answers *185*
Vocubulary Exercise Answers *186*
Progress Chart *187*
Progress Graph *187*
Bibliography *188*
Index *190*

Editor's Foreword

It is a privilege to commend this book to the great army of people, young and old, who are eager to master more knowledge of our exasperating and endearing world – the heritage of the past, scientific and political developments of the day, current and classical literature. It marks the emergence of a brilliant young man, Tony Buzan, whose career I have, in a modest way, been trying to foster for several years and who has rapidly made a name for himself.

Tony Buzan here reduces to a simple and easily followed learning system what I and my contemporaries had to acquire painfully and empirically – if we acquired it at all. Let me assure you that, using this system, you will swiftly equal if not exceed what I have had to do for many years: read at least three newspapers a day; some 25 scientific journals, half a dozen general weeklies and two or three books each week; and about a dozen general magazines each month – as well as many letters, reports, clippings, references, handbooks, catalogues, etc.

I could wish that I had years ago enjoyed the benefit of the system Tony Buzan here sets forth so lucidly. It would have saved me much lost effort, many wasted moves; and I am not a bit ashamed to admit that even today I continue to learn from him how to do still better. You are likely to have the advantage of starting out on the right foot at a much earlier stage. I plead with you to seize the opportunity! It will require effort, even with Tony Buzan's clearly explained step-by-step system; but, if you persevere, you will find that this book is like the opening of a door into a world thick with the golden sunshine of knowledge.

The late Heinz Norden, Erstwhile Information Editor,
The Book of Knowledge,
Fellow of the Institute of Linguistics

Author's Foreword

When I was 14, my class was given a battery of tests to measure our mental skills.

Concealed among them was a speed reading test. A few weeks later we were given our results, and I found that I had scored an average of 213 words per minute (wpm). My first reaction was elation, because 213 sounded like a lot! However, my joy did not last long, for our teacher soon explained that 200 wpm was fairly average, and that the fastest student in the class had scored 314 wpm – just over 100 wpm faster than my average score.

This demoralizing piece of news was to change my life: as soon as the class ended I rushed up to the teacher and asked him how I could improve my speed. He answered that there was no way of doing so, and that your reading speed, like your IQ, your adult height and the colour of your eyes, was fundamentally unchangeable.

This did not quite ring true. Why? I had just started a vigorous phy-sical training programme, and had noticed dramatic changes in nearly every muscle of my body within a few weeks. If knowing the right exercises had enabled me to bring about such physical trans-formation, why shouldn't the appropriate visual and mental exercises allow me to change my reading speed, comprehension and memory of what I had read?

These questions launched me on a search that soon had me cracking the 400 wpm barrier, and eventually reading comfortably at speeds of over 1000 wpm. Through these investigations, I realized that, on all levels, *reading is to the mind as aerobic training is to the body.*

By learning about the miracle of my eyes and the extraordinary capacity of my brain, I not only increased my speed, comprehension and memory; I also found myself able to think faster and more creatively, to make better notes, to pass exams with relative ease, to study more successfully, and to save days, weeks and even months of my time.

The Speed Reading Book, the book you now hold in your hands, is the result of 40 years of practice and research in the field. Its pages contain the essential secrets I have learnt during that time.

I hope you find the journey exciting, and benefit as much from these Mental Literacy techniques as I have done.

Appreciation

I would like to thank especially: Vanda North, my External Editor-in-Chief, whose own speeding 'eagle eye' so successfully helped to give this book its current form; my personal assistants, Lesley Bias, Phyllida Wilson and Sandy Zambaux, whose work in typing the manuscript and helping with the general production of the book was invaluable; Justin Coen for his original work on illustrations and proof reading; the entire Folley family for providing me with the glorious surroundings in which to complete this book; the Buzan Centres and all Radiant Thinking Instructors for their support, research and teaching of these methods; Caro and Peter Ayre for providing the sanctuary of Greenham Hall where much of the early research was completed; Robyn Ponty of Lizard Island, Australia, who similarly provided me with care and sustenance during the gestation period; Sean Adam for his support and dedication to the cause of better reading; 'My Team' at the BBC, Chris Weller, Sheila Ableman; and The Brain Trust and all members of the Brain Clubs for their commitment to the global goal of Mental Literacy and, in particular, to the concept of speed reading.

How to Use The Speed Reading Book

Learning to speed read effortlessly and fluently has been claimed by millions of people around the world to be one of the most rewarding and significant events of their lives.

FOREWORD

This introduction takes you through the **main purposes of *The Speed Reading Book*** and the way the book is structured in five main divisions. It also explains the **organization of each chapter**, and tells you **how to speed read this speed reading course**.

PURPOSES OF THE SPEED READING BOOK

This book has six main purposes:

1 To improve your reading speed dramatically.
2 To maintain and improve your comprehension.
3 To increase your understanding of the function of your eyes and your brain, in order to help you use them far more effectively while reading and studying, and also to use them more effectively in your everyday personal and professional life.
4 To help you improve both your vocabulary and general knowledge.
5 To save you time.
6 To give you confidence.

THE MAIN DIVISIONS

For ease of reading and learning, *The Speed Reading Book* is arranged in five divisions:

Division One – Exploring Your Speeds

In this division you are shown how to use a simple graph to check your own progress in reading-speed and comprehension throughout the book. This division also includes a history of speed reading, a state-of-the-art update on the theory of reading, and a new definition of reading that will help you improve on all levels.

Division Two – Your Amazing Eyes

The Amazing Eyes division helps you to understand that your eyes really *are* amazing, and shows you how to gain control of them in order to immediately increase your reading speed and improve your comprehension. You will be introduced to the current Top Ten speed readers in the world, as well as to some of the great characters who feature in the history of speed reading.

This division also teaches you techniques that will help you to guide your eyes more effectively on the page, to develop advanced skimming and scanning skills, and to arrange your environment in a way that actually helps your eyes and brain read faster.

Throughout this division you are given exercises and speed reading tests that enable you to strengthen the 'muscle' of your eye/brain system, and continue to accelerate your reading speed.

Division Three – Super-Concentration and Comprehension

This division concentrates on the main reading problems and how to overcome them. These include poor concentration and poor compre-hension, sub-vocalization, and 'learning problems' such as dyslexia and ADDS (Attention Deficit Disability Syndrome).

This is a 'good news' division in which you will discover that *all* difficulties can be overcome.

Division Four – Developing Your Advanced Speed Reading Skills

Division Four helps you develop the most important factor in increas-ing your intelligence – your vocabulary. These chapters introduce you to the prefixes, suffixes and roots of tens of thousands of words, the keys that can unlock the doors to universes of vocabulary and under-standing.

This division also explains Mind Mapping® (the new dimension in thinking and note-taking), and shows you how to use your knowledge of paragraph structure to increase your reading effectiveness and how to get a 'bird's eye view' of every book you read.

Division Five – Becoming a Master Reader: Advanced Use of Your Eye/Brain System

In the final division of *The Speed Reading Book* you are introduced to advanced reading practices, including a comprehensive study technique, how to gain control of newspapers and magazines, and how to deal with the information explosion emanating from computer screens and other 'literate machines'. This division also shows you how to apply speed reading techniques to literature and poetry, and introduces the new concept of the 'Knowledge File' – a speed rea-der's method for keeping up to date in any subject area desired.

This division ends with a look into your increasingly bright future, and gives advice on how to continue and improve your reading speed, comprehension, speed reading practices and habits for the rest of your life.

The sections that follow the last division include the Self Test

Answers, your Progress Chart, your Progress Graph, a Bibliography, an Index and information on Buzan Centres.

Please send for a membership application form for the Brain Clubs worldwide, available to anyone who has bought *The Speed Reading Book*.

As a member of the club you will receive the latest information on your brain and how to use it, updates on speed reading news, and contact with thousands of people who share your interests.

The five divisions have been summarized in colour in the Master Mind Maps on Plates I, IV, V, VII, VIII.

ORGANIZATION OF CHAPTERS

The longer chapters in *The Speed Reading Book* contain:
• A foreword introducing the main thrust of the chapter.
• The chapter itself.
• Self-improvement exercises.
• Special readings to help you check your current speed and comprehension.
• Brief summaries.
• An Eye-Cue action plan.
• An Onword linking each chapter with the next.

Self Tests

Seven of the chapters in *The Speed Reading Book* contain a graded series of articles and selected readings which will give you a continuing indication of your progress. The self tests at the beginning of the book are designed to increase your reading speed, those in the middle of the book will develop your powers of perception and vocabulary, and those at the end of the book will enable you to achieve your full speed reading potential.

Some of these reading passages deal with the history and theory of the major areas of human knowledge; others are articles on the latest research into learning and your brain. By the time you finish the book you will therefore not only have increased your reading speed, improved your comprehension and heightened your critical and appreciative abilities; you will also have gained a far wider knowledge of yourself and the universe around you. The seven articles are:

1 The Intelligence War – At the Front with Brain Training
2 Art – Primitive to Christian
3 Animal Intelligence
4 Are We Alone in the Universe? – Extra-Terrestrial Intelligences
5 Baby Brain
6 The Awakening Earth: Our Next Evolutionary Leap – The Global Brain
7 Your Brain – The Enchanted Loom

The Exercises
Seven chapters in *The Speed Reading Book* contain special exercises designed to enhance your visual perception, mental awareness, critical faculties, and the power of your vocabulary.

Like muscle-building exercises, many of them will benefit you even more if you repeat them several times.

All the chapters are interspersed with plentiful illustrations and diagrams to help you understand the content more easily. They also contain stories that will encourage and inspire you.

HOW TO SPEED READ *THE SPEED READING BOOK!*
The Speed Reading Book is a one-week, two-week, three-week or four-week course, depending on how speedily you wish to accomplish your goals!

Read the next few paragraphs, then draw up your study plans.

First, go through the table of contents thoroughly, mapping out the territory you wish to cover. Then roughly plan the time period you will devote to each division of the book, finishing with a general outline in your mind's eye of both the content and your programme of study. This should take only a few minutes.

After this, quickly browse through the entire book, familiarize yourself with the different divisions, and start filling in your mental picture of the 'continent' of the book and your goals.

Now decide whether you wish to complete a chapter a day, or two or three chapters a day, or whether you wish to vary your pace. Once you have made this decision, *record your study plan in your diary, marking the date on which you will begin and the date on which you will finish the book.* When you are calculating this, bear in mind that each chapter is on average only ten pages long, and that most of the exercises will be easy for you to accomplish.

You are about to embark on one of the most exciting journeys of your life – turn the page to begin.

OPENING QUIZ

To stimulate your thinking about reading and speed reading, there follows a quiz on reading habits and skills. Answer yes or no for each of the 20 questions, then turn the page to check your results.

1 Speeds of over 1000 words per minute are possible.   Yes/No

2 For better comprehension you should read slowly and carefully.
Yes/No

3 Word-for-word reading helps comprehension.   Yes/No

4 Sub-vocalization is a reading habit that slows you down and should be reduced or eliminated.   Yes/No

5 You should endeavour to understand 100 per cent of what you read.
Yes/No

6 You should attempt to remember 100 per cent of what you read.
Yes/No

7 Your eye should sweep in a continuous flowing movement along the line as it reads.   Yes/No

8 When you miss something while reading, you should skip back to make sure you understand it before you move on.   Yes/No

9 Reading with your finger on the page slows you down and should be eliminated with training.   Yes/No

10 When you encounter problems of comprehension and understanding in the text, you should work them out before moving on to the following text in order to guarantee your ongoing comprehension. Yes/No

11 A good or important book should be read page by page, never reading page 20 until you have read page 19, and certainly not reading the end before you have completed the beginning.   Yes/No

12 Skipping words is a lazy habit and should be eliminated.   Yes/No

13 When you come to important items in a text you should note them in order to improve your memory.   Yes/No

14 Your level of motivation does not affect the fundamental ways in which eyes communicate with your brain, and does not affect your reading speed.   Yes/No

15 Your notes should always be in a neat, ordered and structured form – mainly sentences and organized lists of the information you have read.   Yes/No

16 When you come to a word that you do not understand, you should have a dictionary close at hand so that you can look it up immediately.

Yes/No

17 One of the dangers of reading faster is that your comprehension is reduced. Yes/No

18 We all read, by definition, at a natural reading speed. Yes/No

19 For novels and poetry, slower reading speeds are important in order to appreciate the meaning of the information and the rhythm of the language. Yes/No

20 You will only truly be able to understand what your eyes focus clearly on. Yes/No

ANSWERS TO OPENING QUIZ

If you have answered only one of these questions with a 'Yes', then you are nearly ready to become one of our speed reading teachers! And that one question was the first – **Speeds of 1000 words per minute are possible.**

All the others should have been answered with a resounding 'No'.

These remaining 19 questions covered the full range of current misconceptions about reading.

If you believe these false assumptions, not only are you believing in something that is not true, you are believing in something that will actively make your reading habits worse and worse, your reading speed slower and slower, and your comprehension and understanding more and more difficult and unsatisfactory.

As you progress through *The Speed Reading Book* these false assumptions will be knocked down one by one, finally leaving you with a clear path on which you can move towards the accomplishment of your own speed reading goals.

CHAPTER ONE

Where are You Now? Check Your Normal Reading Speed and Comprehension

In any learning or self-improvement situation, it is essential to find the true base from which you start. There is no right or wrong, good or bad in this; only an accurate assessment of where you are positioned at present. Whatever that position is, it will form a solid foundation from which you can springboard successfully to your ultimate goal.

FOREWORD

In this chapter I ask you to do exactly the opposite of what I shall be asking you to do in every other chapter. I ask you *not* to speed read, because you need to **calculate your present speed** in order to **judge accurately the progress you make** throughout the book.

Your **comprehension level** will also be tested at the end with 15 multiple-choice and true/false questions. When reading the passage, don't go for very high or very low levels of comprehension; go for *exactly* the same kind of comprehension you would normally expect to get when reading this type of material.

Don't worry about getting low scores in either speed or comprehension. Remember that this book has been written for people who want to improve their reading skills and that low initial scores are not only common, they are expected.

So, no dashing along for higher than usual speeds, no plodding for super comprehension scores, and no worrying about your result. Have your watch by your side, and do your reading privately (someone timing you or watching you inevitably interferes with your comprehension and tends to make some people read more hurriedly than usual, others more slowly).

When you have reached the end of the article, immediately check your watch and calculate your speed. Full instructions will be given on how to do this.

Prepare yourself, and start *a normal* reading of the following passage *now*.

SELF TEST 1   The Intelligence War – At the Front with Brain Training

New World Trends

Stock market analysts watch, like hawks, ten individuals in Silicon Valley. When there is even a hint that one might move from Company A to Company B, the world's stock markets shift.

The English Manpower Services Commission recently published a survey in which it was noted that, of the top 10 per cent of British companies, 80 per cent invested considerable money and time in training; and in the bottom 10 per cent of companies no money or time was invested.

In Minnesota, the Plato Computer Education Project has already raised the thinking and academic performance levels of 200,000 pupils.

In the armed forces of an increasing number of countries, mental martial arts are becoming as important as physical combat skills.

National Olympic squads are devoting as much as 40 per cent of their training time to the development of positive mind set, mental stamina and visualization.

In the Fortune 500 (the 500 top-earning US companies), the top five computer companies alone have spent over a billion dollars on educating their employees, and the development of intellectual capital has become the main priority, including the development of the world's most powerful currency – the currency of intelligence.

In Caracas, Dr Luis Alberto Machado became the first person to be given a government portfolio as Minister of Intelligence, with a political mandate to increase the mental power of the nation.

We are witnessing a quantum leap in human evolution – the awareness by intelligence of itself, and the concommitant awareness that this intelligence can be nurtured to astounding advantage.

This encouraging news must be considered in the context of the most significant problem areas as defined by the business community.

Over the last 20 years over 100,000 people from each of the five major continents have been polled. The top 20 areas commonly mentioned as requiring improvement are:

1 Reading speed
2 Reading comprehension
3 General study skills
4 Handling the information explosion
5 Memory
6 Concentration
7 Oral communication skills
8 Written communication skills
9 Creative thinking
10 Planning
11 Note-taking

12 Problem analysis
13 Problem solving
14 Motivation
15 Analytical thinking
16 Examination techniques
17 Prioritizing
18 Time management
19 Assimilation of information
20 Getting started (procrastination)
21 Mental ability declining with age

With the aid of modern research on the functioning of the brain, each of these problems can be tackled with relative ease. This research covers:

1 The functions of the left and right cortex
2 Mind Mapping
3 Super-speed and range reading/intellectual commando units
4 Mnemonic techniques
5 Memory loss after learning
6 The brain cell
7 Mental abilities and ageing

The Functions of the Left and Right Cortex

It has now become common knowledge that the left and right cortical structures of the brain tend to deal with different intellectual functions. The left cortex primarily handles logic, words, number, sequence, analysis, linearity and listing, while the right cortex processes rhythm, colour, imagination, day-dreaming, spatial relationships and dimension.

What has recently been realized is that the left cortex is not the 'academic' side, nor is the right cortex the 'creative, intuitive, emotional' side. We now know from volumes of research that both sides need to be used in conjunction with each other for there to be both academic and creative success.

The Einsteins, Newtons, Cezannes and Mozarts of this world, like the great business geniuses, combined their linguistic, numerical and analytical skills with imagination and visualization in order to produce their creative masterpieces.

Mind Mapping

Using this basic knowledge of our mental functioning, it is possible to train people in order to solve each of these problem areas, often producing incremental improvements of 500 per cent.

One of the modern methods of achieving such improvements is Mind Mapping.

In traditional note-taking, whether it be for remembering information, for preparing written or oral communication, for organizing your thoughts, for problem analysis, for planning or for creative thinking, the standard mode of presentation is linear: either sentences, short lists of phrases, or numerically and alphabetically ordered lists. These methods, because of their lack of colour, visual rhythm, image and spatial relationships, cauterize the brain's thinking capacities, and literally impede each of the aforementioned mental processes.

Mind Mapping, by contrast, uses the full range of the brain's abilities, placing an image in the centre of the page in order to facilitate memorization and the creative generation of ideas, and subsequently branching out in associative networks that mirror externally the brain's internal structures. Using this approach, you can prepare speeches in minutes rather than days; problems can be solved both morecomprehensively and more rapidly; memory can be improved from absent to perfect; and creative thinkers can generate a limitless number of ideas rather than a truncated list.

Super-Speed and Range Reading/Intellectual Commando Units

By combining Mind Mapping with new super-speed and range reading techniques (which allow speeds of well over 1000 words per minute along with excellent comprehension, and eventual *effective* reading speeds of about 10,000 words per minute), one can form intellectual commando units.

Reading at these advanced speeds, Mind Mapping in detail the outline of the book and its chapters, and exchanging the information gathered by using advanced Mind Mapping and presentation skills, it is possible for four or more individuals to acquire, integrate, memorize and begin to apply in their professional situation four complete books' worth of new information in one day.

These techniques have recently been applied in the multinational organizations Nabisco and Digital Computers. In these instances, 40 and 120 senior executives respectively divided their groups into four. Each individual in each of the four sub-groups spent two hours applying speed and range reading techniques to one of the four selected books.

When the two hours were completed, the members of each sub-group discussed among themselves their understandings, interpretations and reactions to the book. Each sub-group then chose one representative who gave a comprehensive lecture to all the members of the three other sub-groups. This process was repeated four times, and at the end of each day, 40 and 120 senior executives in each company walked out of their seminar room with four complete new books' worth of information not only *in* their heads, but integrated, analysed and memorized.

This approach can be similarly used in the family situation, and is already being used in families around the world.

Recently, a Mexican family applied it to their three children, ranging in age from six to 15 Within two months, each child was the top student in its year, having been able to complete in two days, with the help of the other family members, what the average child/student completes in a year.

Mnemonic Techniques

Mnemonic techniques were originally invented by the Greeks, and were thought to be 'tricks'. We now realize that these devices are soundly based on the brain's functioning, and that, when applied appropriately, they can dramatically improve anyone's memory.

Mnemonic techniques require you to use the principles of association and imagination, to create dramatic, colourful, sensual and consequently unforgettable images in your mind.

The Mind Map is in fact a multidimensional mnemonic, using the brain's inbuilt functions to imprint more effectively data/information upon itself.

Using mnemonics, businessmen have been trained to remember perfectly 40 newly introduced people, and to similarly memorize lists of over 100 products, with relevant facts and data. These techniques are now being applied at the IBM Training Centre in Stockholm, and have had a major impact on the success of their 17-week introductory training programme. The same techniques have been used in the World Memory Championships for the last five years, especially by the reigning World Champion and current record-holder, Dominic O'Brien.

There is an increasing awareness that learning how to learn *before* any other training has been given is good business sense. This is why a number of the more progressive international organizations are now making mnemonics the obligatory 'front end' to all their training courses. Simple calculation shows that, if £1,000,000 is spent on training, and 80 per cent of that training is forgotten within two weeks, £800,000 has been lost during that same period!

Memory Loss After Learning

Memory loss after learning is dramatic.

After a one-hour learning period, there is a short rise in the recall of information as the brain integrates the new data. This is followed by a dramatic decline in which, after 24 hours, as much as 80 per cent of detail is lost.

The scale remains roughly the same regardless of the length of input time. Thus a three-day course is more or less forgotten within one to two weeks of completion.

The implications are disturbing; if a multinational firm spends

$50 million per year on training and there is no appropriate reviewing programmed into the educational structure, $40 million will have been lost with incredible efficiency within a few days of that training's completion.

By gaining a simple understanding of the memory's rhythms, it is possible not only to avert this decline, but also to train people in such a way as to *increase* the amount learnt and retained.

The Brain Cell
In the last five years the brain cell has become the new frontier in the human search for knowledge.

Not only do we each have 1,000,000,000,000 brain cells, but the interconnections between them can form a staggeringly large number of patterns and permutations. This number, calculated by the Russian neuro-anatomist Petr K. Anokhin, is one followed by ten million kilometres of standard typewritten noughts!

With our inherent capacity to integrate and juggle multiple billions of bits of data, it has become apparent to those involved in brain research that adequate training of our phenomenal biocomputer (which can calculate in one second what it would take the Cray computer, at 400 million calculations per second, 100 years to accomplish) will enormously accelerate and increase our ability to problem solve, to analyse, to prioritize, to create and to communicate.

Mental Abilities and Ageing
'They die!' is the usual chorus from people in response to the question: 'What happens to your brain cells as they get older?' It is usually voiced with extraordinary and surprising enthusiasm.

However, one of the most delightful pieces of news from modern brain research comes from Dr Marion Diamond of the University of California, who has recently confirmed that there is no evidence of brain cell loss with age in normal, active and healthy brains.

On the contrary, research is now indicating that, if the brain is used and trained, there is a biological increase in its interconnective complexity, i.e. the person's intelligence is raised.

Training of people in their sixties, seventies, eighties and nineties has shown that, in every area of mental performance, statistically significant and permanent improvements can be made.

We are at the beginning of a revolution the like of which the world has never seen before: the quantum leap in the development of human intelligence.

On the personal front, in education and in business, information from psychological, neuro-physiological and educational laboratories is being used to solve problems which were hitherto accepted as an inevitable part of the ageing process.

By applying our knowledge of the brain's separate functions, by externally reflecting our internal processes in Mind Map form, by making use of the innate elements and rhythms of memory, and by applying our knowledge of the brain cell and the possibilities for continued mental improvement throughout life, we realize that the intelligence war can indeed be won.

****

Stop Your Timer Now
Length of time: 22.... mins

Next, calculate your reading speed in words per minute (wpm) by simply dividing the number of words in the passage (in this case 1871) by the time (in minutes) you took.

Speed Reading Formula:
words per minute (wpm) = $\dfrac{\text{number of words}}{\text{time}}$

When you have completed your calculation, enter the number in the wpm slot at the end of this paragraph, and enter it on your Progress Chart and your Progress Graph on page 187.

Words per minute: .85.04

SELF TEST 1: COMPREHENSION
For each question, either circle 'True' or 'False' or tick the right answer.

1 The top 80 per cent of British companies invest considerable money and time in training.   True/False

2 National Olympic squads are devoting as much as:
(a) 20 per cent
(b) 30 per cent
(c) 40 per cent
(d) 50 per cent
Match their training time to the development of positive mind set, mental stamina and visualization.

3 The first person to be given a government portfolio as Minister of Intelligence was:
(a) Dr Marion Diamond
(b) Dr Luis Alberto Machado
(c) Dominic O'Brien
(d) Plato

4 Number is mainly a left-cortex function.   True/False

5 The Einsteins, Newtons, Cezannes and Mozarts of this world were successful because they *primarily* combined:

(a) number with logic
(b) words with analysis
(c) colour with rhythm
(d) analysis with imagination

6 In Mind Mapping, you:
(a) place an image in the centre
(b) place a word in the centre
(c) place nothing in the centre
(d) always place a word and an image in the centre

7 Using new super-speed and range reading techniques, you should be able to establish new normal speeds of well over:
(a) 500 words per minute
(b) 1000 words per minute
(c) 10,000 words per minute
(d) 100,000 words per minute

8 The two companies who formed intellectual commando units for studying books were:
(a) IBM and Coca Cola
(b) Digital and Nabisco
(c) Nabisco and Microsoft
(d) IBM and ICL

9 Mnemonic techniques were originally invented by:
(a) the Chinese
(b) the Romans
(c) the Greeks
(d) Plato

10 After a one-hour period there is:
(a) a short rise in the recall of information
(b) a levelling off in the recall of information
(c) a short drop in the recall of information
(d) a rapid drop in the recall of information

11 Twenty-four hours after a learning period the following percentage of detail is often lost:
(a) 60 per cent
(b) 70 per cent
(c) 80 per cent
(d) 90 per cent

12 The number of brain cells in the average brain is:
(a) a million
(b) a thousand million
(c) a million million
(d) a thousand million million

13 The Cray computer is finally approaching the capacity of the brain in its overall ability to calculate. True/False

14 Dr Marion Diamond recently confirmed that there is:
(a) no evidence of brain cell loss with age in normal active and healthy brains
(b) no evidence of brain cell loss with age in any brain
(c) no evidence of brain cell loss with age in brains under 40
(d) evidence of slight brain cell loss with age in normal active and healthy brains

15 With adequate training, statistically significant and permanent improvements in intelligence can be made in people up to the age of:
(a) 60
(b) 70
(c) 80
(d) 90

Check your answers against those on page 185. Then divide your score by 15 and multiply by 100 to calculate your percentage comprehension.

Comprehension score: .... out of 15
.... per cent

Now enter your score in your Progress Chart and your Progress Graph on page 187.

HOW DID YOU DO?
Now that you have finished your first Self Test, you will have a base level from which you will *inevitably* improve. To find out where you stand in relation to readers around the world, consult the table below which gives you a range of reading speeds and comprehensions from poor to one-in-a-thousand. You can use this table to help you refine your goals as you progress through the book.

Another interesting set of statistics on reading speeds relates

	Reader	Speed wpm	Comprehension
1	Poor	10–100	30–50%
2	Average	200–240	50–70%
3	Functionally literate	400	70–80%
4	Top 1 in 100	800–1000	80+%
5	Top 1 in 1000	1000+	80+%

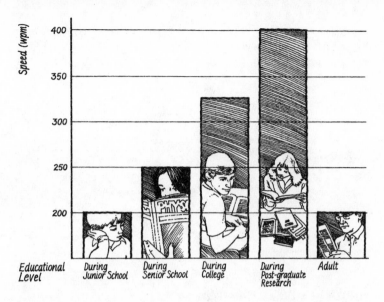

Fig. 1 Graph showing average reading rate for people throughout life. *See text below.*

speed to educational level (see Fig.1, above).

The reason for the increase with education is not so much due to gaining knowledge of how to read better, but to the simple pressure of having to read so much more material in such a compressed time. In other words, motivation is a crucial factor. Further evidence for this is provided by the fact that the adult, after leaving formal education, slips right back to the junior school level, primarily because motivation has declined and the pressure is off. The amount of reading is, on average, reduced to as little as one book per year.

Unlike the individuals surveyed, when you have absorbed the information in this book, you will not fall back to your previous low levels – instead you will maintain and improve whatever level you have achieved.

SUMMARY

- Your reading speed now is: ....
- Your comprehension now is: ....
- The formula for calculating wpm is: number of words
                                        time
- Reading speeds range from 1–1000+ words per minute.
- The average reading speed is 200–220 words per minute.
- The more educated person usually reads faster only because of

pressure of time and greater motivation, not because they know how to read more effectively.
• Everyone (including you) can improve their reading speed and comprehension.

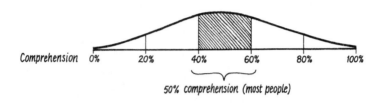

Fig. 2 Speed reading comprehension curve showing comprehension rate for the general population.

HIGH EYE-CUE ACTION POINTS
1 Make sure you have entered your speed and comprehension in your Progress Chart and your Progress Graph on page 187.
2 Check your diary for the date of your next speed reading session.
3 Increase your motivation – it increases your speed.
4 Quickly preview Chapter 2 before you read it.

ONWORD
Now that you have completed the introduction, flipped through all the pages of the book, and completed your first Self Test, there follows a quick overview of the history of speed reading, bringing you up to date with the latest developments in the field, in order to prepare you for your first major leap forward.

CHAPTER TWO

The History of Speed Reading

The search for the secrets to speed reading has lead us to find the answer, surprisingly, not in the eye but in the brain.

FOREWORD
This chapter describes the recent **information explosion**, explores **the methods by which you were probably taught to read**, tells you **the fascinating story of how speed reading developed**, introduces you to **the current world record holders** and their extraordinary speeds, and looks at **your potential to join their ranks**.

THE INFORMATION EXPLOSION
In recent years the volume of magazines and books pouring off the international presses has reached almost unmanageable proportions. Furthermore, the invention of the computer and fax has added, for many people, literally *miles* of extra reading material.

A few decades ago, the average person was able to comfortably navigate the rivers of information. But those rivers have now turned into torrents which threaten to engulf us.

Let us look at the way in which *you* were taught to read, at the historical development of speed reading, and then at your potential to easily 'ride the rapids'!

HOW WERE *YOU* TAUGHT TO READ?
Can you remember by which method you were taught? Was it the phonic method, or the look-say method, or a combination of both?

The Phonic Method
The phonic method first introduces the child to the ordinary alphabet from a to z, and then introduces the sound of each letter so that 'a' becomes 'ah', 'b' becomes 'buh', and so on. The child is then introduced to the letters and sounds in the context of words. Thus 'the cat' will first be read 'tuh-heh-eh kuh-ah-tuh' (not 'see-aye-tee' etc.) until the teacher has moulded the word into its proper form. When the child has learnt to make the correct sounds (vocalizes properly) he is told to read silently. This last stage often takes a long time, and many children and even adults never get past the stage of moving their lips while reading. Those who *do* get past this stage may nevertheless still be vocalizing *to themselves*. That is to say, as they

27

read, they are consciously aware of the sound of each word. This is called *sub-vocalization*.

The Look-Say Method

The look-say method of teaching children to read also relies on a word or verbal response. The child is shown a picture (for example, a cow) with the word that represents the object printed clearly beneath it, thus: **cow**. The teacher then asks the child for the correct response. If the incorrect answer is given (for example 'elephant'!) the teacher guides the child to the correct response and then moves on to the next word. When the child has reached a reasonable level of proficiency he will be in a position similar to the child who has been taught by the phonic method: able to read, still vocalizing, and told that he should read silently.

What is Real Literacy?

Once the child is able to recognize words and to read silently, it is generally assumed that he has learnt to read and is therefore literate. From the age of five to seven onwards, very little further instruction is given, as it is believed that, once the skill of reading has been learnt, the child needs only to apply it.

Nothing could be further from the truth, for what has in fact been taught is the very first stage of reading. Leaving the child in this state, in which it remains until it is an adult, is very much like assuming that, once a baby has learnt to crawl, the process of locomotion is complete! Yet the worlds of walking, running, dancing and related activities have all been left unexplored.

The same applies to reading. We have been left stranded on the floor, now it is time to learn to walk, run and dance!

THE DEVELOPMENT OF SPEED READING

Speed reading originated at the beginning of this century, when the publication explosion swamped readers with more than they could possibly handle at normal reading rates. Most early courses, however, were based on information from a rather unexpected source – the Royal Air Force.

During the First World War air force tacticians had found that, when flying, a number of pilots were unable to distinguish planes seen at a distance. In the life-and-death situation of air combat, this was obviously a serious disadvantage, and the tacticians set about finding a remedy. They developed a machine called a tachistoscope, which flashes images for varying short spaces of time on a large screen. They started by flashing fairly large pictures of friendly and enemy aircraft at very slow exposures and then gradually shortened the exposure, while decreasing the size and changing the angle of the image seen.

To their surprise, they found that, with training, the average person was able to distinguish almost specklike representations of different planes when the images had been flashed on the screen for only *one five-hundredth of a second.*

Reasoning that, if the eyes could see at this incredible speed, reading speeds could obviously be dramatically improved, they decided to transfer this information to reading. Using exactly the same device, they first flashed one word in large type for as long as five seconds on a screen, gradually reducing the size of the word and shortening the length of each flash. Eventually they were flashing four words simultaneously on a screen for one five-hundredth of a second, and the subjects were still able to read them.

As a consequence of these findings, most speed reading courses have been based on this flash-card or tachistoscopic training (also known as still-screen training).

On average, the individual's speeds go from 200 words per minute to 400 words per minute. At first this sounds wonderful: a doubling of reading speed!

However, if you look at the mathematics, it becomes clear that something is drastically wrong. If the eye is able to recognize images (for example, a plane or a word) in *one five-hundredth of a second,* then the expected reading speed in a minute would be *60 seconds x 500 words per second = 30,000* (or a short book) in a minute! Where have the other 29,600 words gone?!

Not realizing this, the tachistoscopic trainers soldiered bravely on. Their approach usually measured the student's progress with a graph graded in units of ten from 100 to 400 words per minute (see Fig.3a, overleaf). With regular training, most people were able to climb from an average of 200 words per minute to an average of 400 per minute, precisely the difference between the junior school student and the post-graduate, as shown on page 25.

The successful tachistoscopic students reported a general dissatisfaction with their results after a few weeks of 'post-graduate reading'. Most reported that, shortly after their course had finished, their reading speed once again sank to its previous level. Again, this is very similar to the reversion to the norm of the standard adult reader (see page 25).

Only recently has it been realized that the *normal range* of reading ability is from roughly 200 to 400 words per minute and that most people operate at the lower end of this range. The increased reading ability observed during the tachistoscopic courses in fact had little to do with the training, but was more due to the students being highly motivated over a period of weeks, and thus being able to reach the top of their normal range. Another explanation for the failure of this approach can be found by referring to the basic rule

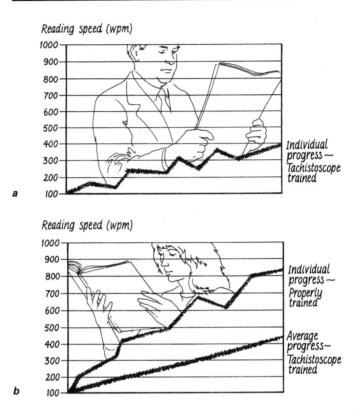

Fig. 3 **a** Tachistoscopic graph **b** Measuring the relative effectiveness of tachistoscopic training against natural reading speeds. *See text on previous page.*

of observation: *in order to see something clearly, your eye must be still in relation to the object it is seeing.*

The Last 30 Years

Although it was gradually realized that the tachistoscope did not provide a *comprehensive* approach to speed reading, the technique became useful as one *part* of a basic training kit.

By the 1960s, researchers – including the American Evelyn Wood – were beginning to discover that, with adequate training, the eyes could learn to move faster, and that comprehension could be maintained above the 400 word-per-minute barrier, which was to speed reading what the four-minute mile once was to athletics.

Various 'dynamic reading schools' sprang up, and the average speed for a good speed reader began to nudge the next Great Barrier – 1000 wpm.

Fuelled by stories of the speed-reading exploits of such public figures as the United States President, John F. Kennedy, the dynamic reading schools flourished, and spawned many variants. Among these was photo-reading, which simply focused on the ability of the eye to 'photograph' larger areas of print than normal.

Entering the Twenty-First Century – Brain Reading

> The revolutionary awareness that this updated edition of *The Speed Reading Book* brings to this field is that it is not primarily the eyes that do your reading for you, it is your *brain*.

This remarkable realization forms the basis for an entirely new approach to this field.

In *The Speed Reading Book* you will be introduced to exercises that allow you to develop the skills of both your eyes and your brain, enabling you to combine the two into a single tool that will make you an intellectual powerhouse.

THE CURRENT WORLD RECORD HOLDERS

At this stage, the reading speeds of the people you are about to 'meet' may seem astounding and totally unattainable. But by the time you have finished this book, you will be lusting after their records!

Speed reading tests are primarily based on the reading of novels. The reader has to read an *entire novel* as fast as possible, subsequently giving a speech to people who have already read the novel in depth. The speech has to include knowledgeable comments about all the following main areas: characters; setting; plot; philosophy; symbolism; language level; literary style; metaphor; themes; historical context. The current Top Ten in the world are as follows:

1	Sean Adam	USA	3850
2	Kjetill Gunnarson	Norway	3050
3	Vanda North	UK	3000
4	Cris van Aken	Netherlands	2520
5	Mithymna Corke	Netherlands	2100
6	Luc van Hof	Netherlands	1906
7	Michael J. Gelb	USA	1805
8	Cinnamon Adam	USA	1782
9	James Longworth	UK	1750
10	Frank van dr Poll	Netherlands	1560

If you are interested in joining this speed reading élite, read this book thoroughly, make sure you practise all the Eye-Cue exercises, join the Brain Club worldwide, send us your top reading speed to date, and make sure you enter the annual World Speed Reading Championships (for more information see page 192).

YOUR SPEED READING POTENTIAL

Your own potential to improve your reading speed to at least double your present rate, and eventually to reach 1000 wpm, is identical to all those in the world's current Top Ten.

Each one of them was a reader who, like you and me, was initially dissatisfied with his or her normal reading speed and decided to put time and effort into developing this most powerful of human skills. *The Speed Reading Book* gives you the perfect opportunity to follow in their eye-steps!

SUMMARY

1 The two main techniques for teaching children to read are the phonic and look-say.

2 These methods only get us to the *first stage* of reading.

3 Speed reading began with the development of speed perception exercises by the Royal Air Force. These tachistoscopic methods enabled people to double their reading speed, but often resulted in a reversion back to normal speeds after a few weeks.

4 Dynamic reading schools broke the 400 wpm barrier.

5 We now know that it is your *brain* that actually does the reading.

6 The Top Ten readers in the world read between 1500 and 3850 wpm.

7 Your potential for improvement is identical to theirs!

HIGH EYE-CUE ACTION POINTS

1 Quickly review, in less than five minutes, everything you have read so far in the book.

2 Check your speed-reading goals, possibly changing them, in view of what you have read in this chapter.

3 Check your diary for the date of the next speed reading session.

4 Spend one minute previewing the next chapter.

ONWORD

Now that you have established your own benchmarks and are familiar with the history of speed reading, you are ready to launch into a definition of the field in which you are about to become an expert.

Reading – A New Definition

Definition is the companion of clarity; clarity is the guide to your goals.

FOREWORD
Ask yourself what reading is, and write your definition in the space below:

Now compare your definition with common ones, such as 'reading is understanding what the author intended', 'reading is taking in the written word' or 'reading is the assimilation of printed information'.

Each of these standard definitions only covers a *part* of the process. An accurate definition must include the *full* range of reading skills.

Chapter 3 **defines reading** in a new way that will enable you to develop all your reading skills.

READING – THE NEW DEFINITION
Reading is actually a seven-part process which comprises the following steps:

1 Recognition
Your knowledge of the alphabetic symbols. This step takes place the instant before physical reading begins.

2 Assimilation
The physical process by which light is reflected from the word; is received by the eye; then transmitted, via the optic nerve, to the brain.

3 Intra-integration
The equivalent of basic comprehension, referring to the linking of all parts of the information being read with all other appropriate parts.

4 Extra-integration
The process in which you bring all of your previous knowledge to

what you read, making appropriate connections, analysing, criticizing, appreciating, selecting and rejecting.

5 Retention
The basic storage of information. Most readers will have experienced entering an examination room, storing most of the required information during the two-hour period and recalling it only as they leave! Storage, then, is not enough, and must be accompanied by recall.

6 Recall
The ability to get back out of storage that which is needed, preferably when it is needed.

7 Communication
The use to which the information is immediately or eventually put. Communication includes written or spoken, as well as representational, including art, dance and other forms of creative expression.

It also includes that vitally important and often neglected human function: thinking! Thinking is your ongoing extra-integration.

In the light of this definition, it can be seen that the common reading and learning problems originally outlined in *Use Your Head:*

vision	fatigue	recall
speed	laziness	impatience
comprehension	boredom	vocabulary
time	interest	sub-vocalization
amount	analysis	typography
surroundings	criticism	literary style
noting	motivation	selection
retention	appreciation	rejection
age	organization	concentration
fear	regression	back-skipping

and the more general learning problems outlined in this book (in Chapter 11) can all be dealt with easily by the reader who has learned to recognize the print and to assimilate, comprehend, understand, retain, recall and communicate.

SUMMARY
1 Reading is a multi-level process.
2 Every level must be developed if you are to become an effective speed reader.

HIGH EYE-CUE ACTION POINTS
1 Rank the seven steps in order, giving the ranking '1' to the step you feel it is most important for you to develop.

2 From the list of reading problems, identify the ones you have and are going to eliminate.

3 Preview the whole of the next division in less than five minutes.

ONWORD

Your knowledge foundations have been laid. You now progress to **Division Two – Your Amazing Eyes**, in which we will explore the use and exercise of the most amazing cameras in the known universe.

CHAPTER FOUR

Gaining Control of Your Eye Movements to Increase Your Speed and Comprehension

Each of your eyes is the most amazing optical instrument known to man, dwarfing by comparison even the most advanced macrocosmos- and microcosmos-searching telescopes and microscopes. The nature of this miraculous instrument can be understood, and, being understood, can be controlled and used to your extraordinary advantage.

FOREWORD
In this chapter we discover some extraordinary facts about your eyes, investigate **how your eyes *really* move when they read**, and introduce you to **five new ways to instantly increase your reading speed and comprehension.**

SOME AMAZING FACTS ABOUT YOUR EYES
Your eyes are one of the wonders of the universe! Consider these amazing facts:

Each of your eyes contains 130 million light receivers. Each light receiver can take in at least five photons (bundles of light energy) per second.

Your eyes distinguish between over ten million different colours.

Acting in harmony, your super light-receivers can decode, in *less than a second*, a scene containing *billions* of pieces of information, with super-photographic accuracy.

The Cerne Laboratory in Switzerland has estimated that it would cost 68 million dollars to build a machine that could duplicate the incredible sophistication of your eyes.

The laboratory also rightly points out that the mechanical 'eye' would be relatively immobile, and nearly the size of a house.

Variations in Pupil Size

We have known for some time that our pupils adjust their size according to light intensity and the nearness of the object. The brighter the light and the nearer the object, the smaller the pupil size.

Western scientists have recently discovered that pupil size also varies with emotion, and that if you are confronted with a sight that especially interests you (like an attractive member of the opposite sex), your pupil size automatically increases. Such changes are small but can be noticed with careful observation. Jade dealers in China have been aware of this for many years. While presenting objects for the customer's inspection, the dealer pays particularly close attention to the customer's eyes, waiting for an increase in pupil size. When this increase has been observed, the dealer knows that the customer is 'hooked' and sets an appropriate price.

As a speed reader, if you are interested in something, your pupil dilates, letting more light in. In other words, the more interested you are, the wider your brain draws the curtains behind your eyes, allowing itself (and you!) to receive, with *no extra effort* more data per second.

Eyes at the Back of Your Head

The phenomenally complex images decoded by your retinal light receivers are sent along the optic nerve (see Plate II) and transmitted to the visual area of your brain – the occipital lobe. The occipital lobe is, paradoxically, not situated just behind the eyes, but at the back of your head. No wonder we describe a very observant person as having eyes at the back of his or her head!

It is the occipital lobe of the brain that actually does the reading, directing your eyes around the page to hunt for information that is of interest to your brain. This knowledge forms the basis of the revolutionary approach to speed reading that will unfold in the next few chapters.

Knowing these amazing new facts about the eyes, it becomes clear that traditional reading habits and reading speeds must be a product of mistraining and misuse; and that if our eyes were understood and trained properly their functions would significantly improve.

HOW DO YOUR EYES REALLY READ?

The answer is that the eyes make small and fairly regular 'jumps'. These take the eye from fixation point to fixation point, usually a bit more than a word at a time. So to sum up, the eye does not move smoothly over the page at all. Instead it moves in small hops from left to right, pausing for a moment to take in a word or two before moving on and repeating the process (see Fig.4a, page 39).

While the eye is moving and pausing, moving and pausing in this way, the information is absorbed *only during the pauses*. These pauses take up most of the time. And, as each pause may last between a quarter and one and a half seconds, it is possible to make an immediate improvement in your reading speed by spending less time on each pause.

Figure 4b opposite shows the eye movements of a very poor reader. This reader makes about twice as many pauses or *fixations*, as they are commonly called, as are required for good comprehension. Extra pauses are caused because the slow reader often re-reads words, sometimes skipping back as many as three places to make sure that the correct meaning has been taken in. These habits of back-skipping (returning, almost as a habit, to words that have just been read) and regression (returning consciously to words which the reader feels have been missed or misunderstood) cause the poor reader's excessive number of fixations.

Research has shown that, in 80 per cent of cases, when readers were not allowed to back-skip or regress, they discovered that their eye had actually taken in the information, and they absorbed it as they read the next few phrases. The speed reader very rarely indulges in these unnecessary repetitions, which dramatically reduce the slow reader's speed. If each back-skip or regression takes roughly a second, and as little as two are made per line, then on an average page of 40 lines, *one minute and 20 seconds* are wasted. On a normal book of 300 pages, *one minute 20 seconds x 300 pages = 400 minutes = 6 2/3 hours* of extra wasted time spent reading (and *not* comprehending)!

THE SPEED READER

Figure 4c opposite shows that the good or speed reader, while not back-skipping nor regressing, also has longer jumps. The good reader also takes in not one word per fixation, but three, four or five.

If we assume for the moment that each fixation takes the same time, and set that time at an average of half a second per fixation, an interesting picture emerges. On a normal line of 12 words per line, the poor reader, fixating on one word per fixation and back-skipping or regressing twice, will take 1/2 + 1/2 + 1/2 + 1/2 + 1/2 + 1/2 + 1/2 + 1/2 + 1/2 + 1/2 + 1/2 + 1/2 + 1/2 + 1/2 = 7 seconds; whereas the speed reader, taking in three and four words per fixation with no back-skipping or regression, takes 1/2 + 1/2 + 1/2 + 1/2 = 2 seconds.

The speed reader, with a minor adjustment in the mechanics of the eye, has out-read and out-sped the slow reader by 350 per cent!

Comprehension

'But wait,' you say. 'I have always been told that for good comprehension I must read "slowly and carefully". Surely increasing my speed will *decrease* my comprehension?'

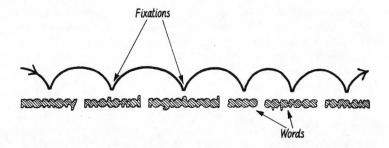

Fig. 4a Diagram of the eye's basic progression while reading. *See page 37.*

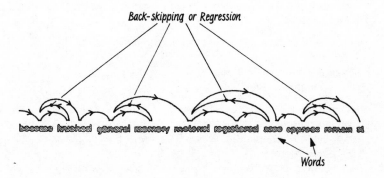

Fig. 4b Diagram of a poor reader's eye movements. *See opposite.*

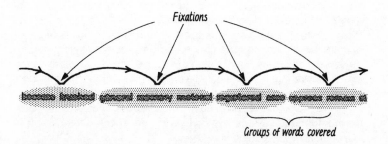

Fig. 4c Diagram of a good reader's eye movements. *See opposite.*

This assumption sounds logical, yet a little investigation shows it to be completely false. Research is increasingly showing that *the faster you read, the better your comprehension.*

To check this for yourself, read the following statement exactly as it is laid out, taking it in 'slowly and carefully' and going for maximum comprehension:

Speed read ing has be en found to be bet ter for under stand ing than slow read ing.

Difficult? Of course! Because your brain is not designed to read at such a disastrously slow pace. Reading slowly and carefully encourages the brain to read more and more slowly, with less and less comprehension and more and more agony.

Now look at the next sentence, this time reading the words as they are grouped:

It has been discovered   that the human brain   with the help of its eyes   takes in information   far more easily when the information   is conveniently grouped in meaningful bundles.

Your brain works far more comfortably at speeds of 400 wpm and above (it is interesting to note that, when most people estimate their reading speed the speed at which they move their finger is in fact 400 wpm or more).

An increase in speed therefore automatically leads to an increase in comprehension. This is because the information is organized in meaningful chunks that make immediate sense to your brain.

This increased ability to understand in turn helps you to remember better, because memory is also based on your brain's ability to organize information in meaningful chunks.

Your first task, then, is to work at eliminating the bad habits of back-skipping, regression, and taking in too few words per fixation.

In addition to getting rid of these bad habits, there is a fourth major way of increasing your speed. If your normal fixation time is one second per fixation, and you can increase your speed to *half a second* per fixation (which should be easy, remembering that your eye can take in information at *one five-hundredth of a second)* then you will have doubled your reading speed.

PERCEPTION EXERCISE 1
The exercise that follows is designed to help you make quicker fixations and take in more information per 'visual gulp'. This should give you the confidence and increased motivation you need to eliminate back-skipping and regression. It will also encourage you to take in more-at-a-glance as you read.

The exercise has been designed for those who favour either the left or the right hand. Use a card to cover up the numbers. Expose each number *as briefly as possible*, giving yourself no more than a split second to see it. Almost at the same time as it is *un*covered it should be *re*covered.

Then write in the space next to the number what you think that number is, and check to see whether you were right or wrong. Continue to the next number, moving from column to column, re-peating the process until the page has been completed. You will find that the exercise becomes more challenging as you progress, because the number of digits is gradually increased. If you can reach the end of the six-digit numbers with few mistakes you will have done extremely well.

You will find that, with practice, you will be able to complete the six-digit numbers in one flash, and this will give you increased confidence to take in two or more words at a time as you read. The numbers that follow include just enough examples of each digit-grouping to allow your eye/brain to get accustomed to that level before moving you on to the next.

...............26.....................	.....................53....................
...............74.....................	.....................79....................
...............82.....................	.....................63....................
...............91.....................	.....................73....................
...............22.....................	.....................53....................
...............35.....................	.....................29....................
...............66.....................	.....................24....................
...............25.....................	.....................31....................
...............46.....................	.....................02....................
...............13.....................	.....................85....................
...............72.....................	.....................43....................
...............20.....................	.....................67....................
...............50.....................	.....................76....................
...............23.....................	.....................06....................
...............40.....................	.....................28....................
...............96.....................	.....................88....................
...............77.....................	.....................84....................
...............45.....................	.....................15....................
...............21.....................	.....................60....................
...............83.....................	.....................49....................
...............99.....................	.....................78....................
...............58.....................	.....................87....................
...............18.....................	.....................03....................
...............277.....................	.....................864....................
...............833.....................	.....................825....................

41

013	953
736	425
226	736
129	490
903	363
271	646
736	726
813	411
413	361
908	058
862	864
832	956
864	525
865	737
837	635
747	737
109	107
251	747
982	837
825	215
211	847
267	880
837	626
108	103
411	217
716	870
975	544
779	656
744	458
764	168
216	562
077	641
865	655
877	668
755	302
866	110
199	617
8638	7475
7875	7356
1178	1088
2277	2436
7426	8656
7655	6423
7777	6555
5433	6545

7657	5433
9880	8702
8612	0188
9871	0677
8766	3343
3777	2244
7544	7702
1074	7653
7654	7623
8764	5433
5325	6543
6423	7056
0653	8765
8644	7655
6118	1154
7703	8674
5423	7534
8762	5734
8277	7374
7272	8862
0177	1761
8767	2345
7654	5433
6511	6531
1075	7120
9841	1106
3753	2754
8297	1173
9275	4828
5702	8567
3089	9861
2850	8422
76542	46533
75252	64322
19866	98011
44904	66255
37621	64533
95412	27549
95339	86422
15155	08436
85369	18643
36438	74323
47721	52741
76201	79285
51915	29477

68224	13655
01678	29371
82102	35727
44627	64652
50664	45610
27392	82547
99266	21420
56439	47539
14733	49763
38657	95079
63644	91637
30080	26091
17533	14161
16843	08222
93867	49653
84611	42983
12548	60258
62938	46104
47250	51252
52952	83704
07650	15733
29332	62969
345783	987104
201896	916846
456782	376520
569832	238755
387513	452876
984764	045018
298436	112785
090769	234743
954137	564220
759484	887632
656892	876926
332558	031410
476831	517195
219575	376490
857393	438753
386280	875316
619474	219564
219575	376982
487615	085377
764973	387520
114874	978564
576330	103866
657894	984372

.............349715.............	.............769103.............
.............496511.............	.............041673.............
.............392588.............	.............643192.............
.............567682.............	.............638726.............
.............284191.............	.............116794.............
.............767936.............	.............436795.............
.............432615.............	.............998665.............
.............816155.............	.............654732.............
.............764130.............	.............284938.............
.............084503.............	.............563982.............
.............278402.............	.............876944.............
.............801019.............	.............932548.............
.............342988.............	.............478902.............
.............865014.............	.............543790.............
.............987655.............	.............037686.............
.............765839.............	.............258765.............
.............965411.............	.............423699.............
.............356794.............	.............175894.............
.............763297.............	.............538722.............
.............090808.............	.............443245.............
.............578392.............	.............121377.............
.............578343.............	.............987532.............
.............013677.............	.............467832.............
.............284680.............	.............538763.............
.............998577.............	.............105790.............
.............334877.............	.............857644.............
.............876653.............	.............664893.............
.............189568.............	.............356543.............
.............987564.............	.............467558.............
.............958747.............	.............465379.............
.............836753.............	.............556794.............
.............001579.............	.............567833.............
.............378696.............	.............189696.............
.............276460.............	.............354673.............
.............287655.............	.............801568.............
.............765844.............	.............968477.............

Now move on to Self Test 2 – Art. Apply all you have learnt in this chapter, eliminating back-skipping and regression, fixating for shorter periods of time, and taking in larger groups of words per fixation. Make sure you start your timer as you commence your reading and stop it the instant you have completed the reading.

The Plus One Rule

The Plus One Rule is simply the following: whenever you are consciously attempting to read faster, aim to read at least one word per minute faster than your previous highest speed. In this way you will not put unnecessary stress on yourself, and you will often find that you have increased by ten or more words per minute, thus comfortably beating your goal, which leads to increasing confidence as well as faster and more efficient reading.

During the Self Test that follows, and each of the subsequent Self Tests, give yourself a Plus Ten Rule, in which your goal is to increase by ten words per minute.

SELF TEST 2   Art – Primitive to Christian

Introduction

Art is one of the most profound expressions of the human brain. From the beginning of history, the mind behind the hand, behind the brush, was engaged in one of the most sophisticated and intricate forms of analysis and expression imaginable. The following sections cover what I believe to be some of the most exciting periods in the history of art.

Primitive Art

All the arts have their origins in prehistoric times, but the representations of animals incised on ivory and bone, or drawn and painted on the walls and ceilings of caves in the north of Spain and south of France, still excite wonder by their exceptional power and apparent 'modernity'. Many masterpieces were produced between roughly 40,000 BC and 10,000 BC. What we notice in the photographs or outline copies made from them is the way in which the artists have selected and emphasized the main characteristics of animals – mammoth and bison, deer, wild boar and wild horse; the knowledge they display of their anatomy; and the skill with which they convey the solid bulk and vigorous movements of the animals, using no more than a little black and red ochre.

There are comparable paintings and drawings by people living a similar life at a much later date. Thus the African Bushmen have left, in rock shelters, drawings of animals as beautiful as those of our first European artists and resembling them in style, though some were done as recently as the nineteenth century. In the next stage of civilization, hunting becomes less important and social life takes a more definite form. Tools of stone and bronze are perfected, the crafts of pottery and weaving are pursued and, with the growth of agriculture, various rites and ceremonies propitiating the elements come into being. The typical primitive society, of which there still remain a few examples, as in Polynesia, is largely concerned in the arts with its rudimentary religion. Carving and sculpture exceed painting in importance: the idol in three dimensions is thought to represent, more impressively, the powers assumed to affect primitive life. Painting and drawing became a series of signs and symbols.

The Ancient Mediterranean World

Painting and drawing in the ancient Mediterranean world has three aspects. First, there is wall painting, with its bold outlines and flat colour, the technique somewhat resembling that of certain modern posters. The ancient Egyptians used it on the exteriors of their temples: a sharply defined low relief providing an outline which was filled with bright colour. The majority of surviving Egyptian paintings are those found on tomb walls, including scenes from the life of the deceased. A number of artistic conventions are regularly used. For example, the male figure is painted in red ochre, the female in yellow; and the head and legs are always in profile however the rest of the body is turned. A great quality is the lively observation of the artists when painting scenes of banqueting and dancing or fishing and fowling along the Nile. The wall paintings of the Minoans of ancient Crete discovered in the palace of Knossos can be likened to those of Egypt with their bright, flat colours and decided outlines, though they are entirely secular in character.

The painted pottery of ancient Greece offers, on a small scale, other examples of these artistic traditions. The male figure is dark, the female figure light; and outline plays a major part. The Greek vase painters (who often signed their cups and vases) can be studied as brilliant draughtsmen with a most exquisite sense of the value of line and silhouette.

In the Classical period, however, the art of vase painting ceased to occupy an important place, and it is now that we first come upon the record of pictures in the modern sense, though our idea of them is unfortunately not based on the authentic works of the legendary masters, Zeuxis and Apelles, but on copies of Greek paintings discovered when the Roman cities Pompeii and Herculaneum were excavated.

It is clear, however, that the Greek painters had given their art a scope and character undreamed of by the Egyptians and Minoans. Their work was no longer flat, but represented light and shade. The Greeks conceived dramatic compositions; they interested themselves in the problem of giving individual character and expression to their figures, in features and gesture. The Greco-Roman works that adorned the villas of wealthy Romans in the first century AD provide examples of landscape (previously unknown) and of still life studied for its own sake. They were the precursors to the later development of painting in Italy.

Byzantine Art

The dissolution of the Roman Empire, the establishment of a new Rome in the former Byzantium (Constantinople), and the emergence of Christianity as the universal creed of the West gave painting a new character, spirit and aim. The Christian religion became the artist's theme. A formal style, now known as Byzantine, suited to express its earnestness and ritual, grew up. Constantinople had many links with the East, whose influence is to be seen in the use of rich colour and geometric patterns.

The main triumphs of Byzantine pictorial art were achieved in mosaic used to decorate the walls or the inner domes of Byzantine churches. Its other forms were, firstly, the icon, the image of Christ or the Virgin, represented in a fixed convention which in itself declared the unalterable nature of belief; and, secondly, the illumination of manuscript Gospels and liturgical works with painting and gold leaf. The style of these is as unchanging as that of the icon.

The Byzantine capital remained intact, prosperous and fixed in its ways for 1100 years after its foundation in the fourth century AD, so that works very similar in many respects may vary considerably in date. The sphere of Byzantine art corresponds to the sphere of influence of the Byzantine Empire: the eastern shores of the Mediterranean, Greece and the Greek islands. To some extent it was carried westward, with the movements of Byzantine missionaries and craftsmen. The style of the famous eighth-century Irish manuscript, the Book of Kells, has links with those of the eastern Mediterranean. The Italian cities of Florence, Siena and Pisa had a Byzantine tradition, the end of which is marked by the paintings of Cimabue in Florence and Duccio in Siena in the thirteenth century. In eastern Europe, what is now Croatia has remarkable Byzantine wall paintings of the twelfth to fourteenth centuries. Greek painters introduced the icon into Russia and the Russian artist Andrew Roublev (c.1360–c.1430) brought the style to a magnificent pitch of development. Crete remained a centre until the sixteenth century and there is still a trace of the Byzantine tradition in the paintings of El Greco (c.1545–1614).

Early Christian Art in the West

East or West, early Christian art generally avoided the realistic depiction of the human form which had been a feature of Classical art. Yet it was not necessarily crude and imperfect, but more spiritual and abstract, in the sense of being removed from mundane affairs; and, from this point of view, it is nowadays judged more favourably than it used to be.

Early Christian art in the West has a complex history. It began by following the Greco-Roman tradition, as in the paintings found in the

Roman catacombs. It was then modified by the local character of the various regions into which the Roman Empire was divided. It was affected by its links, religious and commercial, with the Eastern Empire. For a long time the monastic art of the illuminated manuscripts was the main form of pictorial art, as in Celtic and Anglo-Saxon Britain and in the empire of Charlemagne.

Two things gradually became clear: Christianity was the one unifying and educational force in Europe; and pictures were the principal means of conveying its message effectively and universally among people who spoke in different tongues or who were unable to read and write. With the great period of church building, which began in the eleventh century, the international Western style known as Romanesque developed. Its greatest products were the wall paintings in churches. Working on a large area, the painters developed a bold and simple style of much grandeur.

Modern Art and Beyond

The French artist Cezanne, known as the Father of Modern Art, took art one step further. He was primarily interested not in *what* he saw, but *how* he saw. He therefore began exploring the way in which light bounces off an object and is received by the human eye/brain. He would look at objects and paint on his canvas only the small planes of light and colour that he saw, gradually building the picture up – very much like a jigsaw puzzle – until the real image emerged.

From Cezanne's work the entire school of Cubism emerged, in which artists not only painted the planes of light, they also painted into the image what they remembered from different perspectives. Thus a human form, in the mind of the artist, could become a composite of that form seen from all angles. In this way their paintings became 'images from the mind' rather than simply images from reality.

Artists such as Wassily Kandinsky and Lorraine Gill have researched even more deeply how and what we see, by examining the relationship between colour and colour, line and line, and line and colour.

In the twenty-first century we are likely to see the development of new theories in art that link it far more closely with mathematics, physics and all the other sciences.

****

Stop Your Timer Now
Length of time: .... mins

Next, calculate your reading speed in words per minute (wpm) by simply dividing the number of words in the passage (in this case 1570) by the time (in minutes) you took.

Speed Reading Formula:

words per minute (wpm) = number of words
time

When you have completed your calculation, enter the number in the wpm slot at the end of this paragraph, and enter it on your Progress Chart and your Progress Graph on page 187.

Words per minute: ....

SELF TEST 2: COMPREHENSION

1 All the arts have their origins in:
(a) Africa
(b) prehistoric times
(c) the early Iron Age
(d) the Nile Delta

2 As far as we currently know, the first artistic 'masterpieces' were produced between:
(a) 100,000 and 50,000 BC
(b) 50,000 and 40,000 BC
(c) 40,000 and 10,000 BC
(d) 10,000 and 5,000 BC

3 The African Bushman, unlike the caveman, did not concern himself so much with animals.   True/False

4 A typical primitive society is largely concerned in its arts with:
(a) painting
(b) hunting
(c) religion
(d) war

5 Ancient Mediterranean wall painting is distinguished by:
(a) fine outlines and brilliant colours
(b) fine outlines, flat colour
(c) bold outlines, brilliant colour
(d) bold outlines, flat colour

6 In Egyptian paintings on tomb walls, the female figure is normally painted in:
(a) red ochre
(b) yellow
(c) brown
(d) red

7 Our first record of pictures in the modern sense is based on:
(a) the authentic works of Zeuxis and Apelles

(b) the great Greek vase painters
(c) copies of Greek paintings found in the Roman cities of Pompeii and Herculaneum
(d) the Italian Rennaissance

8 The first examples of landscape were found:
(a) when excavating Greek cities
(b) in the Egyptian tombs
(c) in the villas of wealthy Romans
(d) in the work of the Minoans

9 In Byzantine art Christianity was the artist's main theme.

True/False

10 The main triumphs of Byzantine pictorial art were achieved in:
(a) mosaic
(b) vases
(c) carpets
(d) depictions of the triumph of the Byzantine Empire

11The icon was a fixed convention in Byzantine art.   True/False

12 The Byzantine school of art lasted approximately:
(a) 110 years
(b) 500 years
(c) 1000 years
(d) 1100 years

13 Early Christian art:
(a) copied Classical art
(b) avoided the realistic depiction of the human form
(c) enhanced the representation of the human form
(d) was not interested in the human form

14 The father of modern art was:
(a) Duccio
(b) El Greco
(c) Cezanne
(d) Picasso

Check your answers against those on page 185.
Then divide your score by 15 and multiply by 100 to calculate
your percentage comprehension.

Comprehension score: .... out of 15
.... per cent

Now enter your score on your Progress Chart and your Progress Graph on page 187.

SUMMARY

1 Your eyes read in stops, or fixations, which take between a quarter and one and a half seconds.

2 The slow reader takes in an average of one word per fixation.

3 The average speed reader takes in three to five words per fixation.

4 Back-skipping and regression are unnecessary.

5 Reading slowly and carefully hinders comprehension.

6 Reading faster and in meaningful chunks improves comprehension.

HIGH EYE-CUE ACTION POINTS

1 Reduce your back-skipping and regression. Move forward only.

2 Shorten the length of time for each fixation.

3 Take in words in large, meaningful chunks.

4 Stay focused.

5 Increase your motivation.

6 At some time in the near future repeat Perception Exercise 1.

7 Quickly preview Chapter 5.

ONWORD

Having completed the first major chapter on improving the mechanics of your eyes, it is clear that, with some basic knowledge, extraordinary increases can be made in your reading speed. This is the first of four such chapters, each of which will enable you to make similarly dramatic improvements. Before moving on to the remaining three, it is essential to provide your eyes and brain with a reading environment that encourages excellence and success. This is the subject of the next chapter.

CHAPTER FIVE

Eye-Deal External and Internal Environmental Speed Reading Conditions

A positive internal environment will interact synergistically (1+1 = 2, 3, 5 +) with a positive external environment to create even more positive effects. A negative internal environment will similarly react synergistically with a negative external environment to create even more negative effects. It is essential to understand this principle, and to apply the first of the two formulae.

FOREWORD

Chapter 5 looks at ways in which we can increase our reading speed and comprehension by **creating the right external conditions**, paying attention to factors such as posture and lighting. This chapter also discusses how to **avoid internal interference** caused by problems like anxiety and ill-health.

CREATING THE BEST EXTERNAL CONDITIONS

Placement and Intensity of Light

The best light to study under is daylight, so, where possible, your desk or reading platform should be placed near a window. If this is

Fig. 5 Diagram showing the best posture and correct position of light source for reading. *See pages 53–6.*

not possible, and at times of day when it is too dim, light should come over your shoulder opposite the hand with which you write, to avoid glare and shadow (see Fig.5 on previous page). Desk lamps can cause eye strain if they are not positioned properly. The light should be bright enough to illuminate adequately the material being read, and should not be so bright as to form a great contrast with the rest of the room. In other words, it's not advisable to huddle up to a bright lamp which beams directly on to the book. In addition to the desk lamp, it is best to have balanced general illumination.

Availability of Materials
So that your brain can 'settle in' comfortably, your study environment should have all the materials you need conveniently placed and easily accessible. Not only will this improve your concentration and comprehension, it will also be a psychological boost. Knowing that your materials are pleasingly and functionally placed increases your enjoyment of the task at hand and makes it easier for you to perform it.

Physical Comfort
Do not make yourself too comfortable! Many people look for the most comfortable and inviting easy-chair in the house, pad it even further with soft cushions, place a footrest in front of it so that they can stretch out more comfortably, prepare a hot drink or open a couple of cans of beer, and then settle down to two hours of intensive work – only to find two hours later that they have been dozing throughout!

Ideally your chair should be neither too hard nor too soft, should have a straight back (a sloping one causes bad posture and back strain and makes proper note-taking uncomfortable) and should in general make you neither too relaxed nor too tense. The chair should support you and encourage good posture.

Height of Chair and Desk
The height of both your chair and your desk are important: the chair should be high enough to allow your thighs to be parallel with the floor or slightly raised from parallel. This will ensure that the main pressure for seating is taken by the main sitting bones at the base of the hips. Sometimes a small stool or telephone directory can help to raise the feet to a comfortable level. A common desk height is 73–81 cm (29–32 inches) and on average the desk should be approximately 20 cm (8 inches) above the seat of the chair.

Distance of the Eyes from the Reading Material
The distance of the eyes from the reading material should be approximately 50 cm (20 inches), a natural distance if one sits as described above. Keeping the reading material this far away makes it much

easier for the eyes to focus on groups of words (see the discussion of peripheral vision on page 75). It also considerably lessens eye strain and the possibility of headaches from reading. To prove this for yourself, try looking at your forefinger when it is almost touching your nose and then look at your whole hand when it is about 46 cm (18 inches) away from you. You will notice a real physical strain in the former and a considerable easing of that strain in the latter, even though you are 'taking in' more.

Posture

Ideally both your feet should be flat on the floor. Your back should be upright and you should aim to gently lengthen your musculature. The slight curves in your back give you essential support. If you try to sit up so that your back is 'too straight', or try to flatten these curves, you will end up feeling exhausted.

If you are sitting on a chair or stool and are reading rather than writing, you may find it more comfortable to hold the book in your hands. Alternatively, if you do prefer to lean a few degrees forward over a desk or table, try resting the book on something so that it is at a slight angle. Above all, make sure that you are sitting on a firm base. Anything soft or too comfortable, like a cushion which gives way, will ultimately send you to sleep!

Sitting in the correct position for reading means that:

• **Your brain receives the maximum flow of air and blood**. When the upper spine and especially the neck are bent into a curve, both your windpipe and the main arteries and veins in your neck are constricted. When you sit up straight the flow opens and your brain can operate at peak efficiency.

• **The flow of electrical energy up your spinal column will maximize the power of your brain**. Adopting an upright stance, while maintaining the slight, natural curves in the spine, has been proven to give the spinal column more power and springiness. Lower back pain and shoulder-aches are also reduced by upright posture.

• **When your body is alert your brain is alert**. When your body is erect your brain knows that something important is happening. When your body is bent forward or slumped over it is telling your brain – through the inner ear and the balance mechanisms – that it is time for sleep, especially when your head is tilted too far from the vertical.

• **Your eyes can make full use of both your central and peripheral vision**. They should be at least 50 cm (20 inches) from the written material.

The height of your chair and desk, the distance of your eyes from the reading material, your physical comfort and your posture are all intimately interlinked. Figure 5 on page 53 shows an ideal situation.

Environment

Your environment will affect your achievements. The place in which you read should be light, spacious, pleasing to the eye, well organized for reading purposes, decorated to your taste, and a place to which you would want to go even when you are not reading.

Because reading, learning and studying have for so long been associated with hard work and punishment, many people make their study area bare, dull and dimly lit, and furnish it with the poorest quality desk and chair. Don't make your study environment into a prison cell, make it a paradise!

If you doubt the importance of this, consider how you feel inside (internal environment) when a special friend greets you warmly and invites you into a delightfully prepared room (external environment). That is the feeling you need to create for and in yourself as you think about the place where you go to read or study. It should invite and welcome you.

AVOIDING INTERNAL INTERFERENCE

Timing

This often makes the difference between completely understanding what you read and completely failing to understand it. Because of habits formed at school many people have never tried to find the times of day at which they do their best reading or learning.

It is vital to experiment with reading at different times, for we all have different peaks and slumps in this regard. Some people find that they study best between five and nine in the morning. Others find they can study only at night, and still others that periods in the late morning or early afternoon are best. If you suspect that bad timing may be the cause of your inability to concentrate and comprehend, experiment as soon as possible.

Interruptions

Just as unknown words and difficult concepts break the flow of concentration and understanding, so do telephone calls, unnecessary breaks, loud noises, and lesser diversions like transistor radios, doodle pads and other items of fidgety interest that often litter a desk, and your air space.

Similarly, your own internal environment can distract you. If you are worrying about personal problems, or you are in some form of physical or mental discomfort, or generally off-colour, concentration and comprehension can be significantly reduced. Note that if your posture is correct your breathing will be deep and relaxed which will, in turn, make you feel more relaxed.

The solution is to make your study environment sacrosanct, and to arrange it so that it supports you. Little things, such as putting the phone on an answering service, having a humorous sign on the door requesting no interruptions, possibly selecting appropriate music, and getting rid of unnecessary distractions will all help. Also, try to make sure that your general life is more in order, and your reading, learning, understanding and memory will all improve. For more information on creating a good study environment, see page 53.

Health Problems
If you are going to undertake an extensive reading or studying programme, you should do everything possible to make sure that your physical resources are adequate to the task. Even such minor illnesses as colds and headaches will make a big difference to your intellectual performance. If you have such symptoms semi-chronically, ask your doctor or health expert for advice. It is particularly useful, in conjunction with medical advice, to start a gentle and consistent exercise programme (see *Buzan's Book of Genius*).

SUMMARY
Your environment is a major factor in improving or reducing your reading speed and comprehension. It is essential to make sure that *every* aspect of your environment, both external and internal, is structured to maximize mental performance.

HIGH EYE-CUE ACTION POINTS
1 Pay immediate attention to your external conditions, especially the lighting, the position of your desk and reading materials, and your posture.
2 Experiment to find the best time of day for *you* to read and learn well.
3 Make sure that your internal environment is calm, peaceful, alert and conducive to study.

ONWORD
Having learnt how your eyes work, and found out how to improve the environment in which they work so that they can work even better, you are now ready to take the next major step forward: doubling what you have already accomplished by means of a revolutionary new reading technique.

CHAPTER SIX

Guiding the Eyes – A New Speed and Range Reading Technique

In the mental arena it is often the first step that is the most difficult. Successive steps become successively more easy. Each advance is a greater advance than the previous advance. The more you learn, the easier it is for you to learn more.

FOREWORD

In this chapter, we **discuss the eyes need for a 'guide' when reading, and learn how best to use such a guide**. This technique 'in one fell swoop' reduces back-skipping and regression, improves speed and comprehension, allows you to expand the number of words taken in per fixation, and is far more relaxing for your eyes.

WHO IS RIGHT – THE BABY OR THE EDUCATIONAL SYSTEM?

When a baby or young child is first learning to read, what is one of the first things he physically does?

He places his finger on the page.

We immediately tell the child to take his finger off the page, because we 'know' that this technique slows him down.

Why, though, does the child do it in the first place?

To maintain focus and aid concentration.

Are we being logical, therefore, when we tell the child to remove the finger? For surely, if the finger *were* slowing the child down, the logical response, in order to enable him to maintain his focus and concentration, would be to ask him to speed the finger up!

Let us delve more deeply into this subject by asking the following questions:

Do you ever use your finger, your thumb, a pencil or pen or any other form of visual guide when you are:

1 looking up a number in a telephone directory	Yes/No
2 looking for a word in a dictionary	Yes/No
3 looking up an item of information in an encyclopaedia or reference work	Yes/No
4 adding up a column of numbers	Yes/No
5 focusing on a point you are about to note	Yes/No

6 showing someone else a point on a page to which you wish them
to pay attention   Yes/No
7 reading normally   Yes/No

Most people will answer 'Yes' to at least half of these questions, and
many 'Yes' to all of them except the last one.

Isn't it extraordinary that we all use guides when we are reading in
virtually every situation *except* normal reading where we have
been specifically instructed *not* to do that to which we are naturally
inclined.

Indeed, the prejudice is so deeply ingrained that if you walked into
a senior professional's office and saw him reading a book using his
finger, you would immediately downgrade your opinion of his intelligence!

So, what is the truth of the matter? Is it better to read with a guide
or without a guide?

Let us find out by means of an experiment.

The Experiment
This two-part experiment is best done with a partner.

In the first part of the experiment, you both sit facing each other,
approximately 60 cm (2 feet) apart, with your arms folded and your
heads still.

Now one partner imagines a perfect circle approximately 46 cm
(18 inches) in diameter. The imaginary circle should be about 30 cm
(12 inches) in front of the eyes. The person who is imagining the
circle follows its outline exactly with his eyes, both partners keep
their arms folded, and the second partner looks very closely at the
first partner, to see exactly *what the partner's eyes are doing*.

The partner who is imagining the circle should be feeling what it is
like to move the eyes perfectly around its circumference.

Do not exchange any information about what you have seen or
experienced at this stage.

Now simply reverse the roles, with the second partner imagining
the circle and following it with the eyes, while the first partner
watches their movement. When you have completed the exercise,
exchange information on what you both saw in your partner's eyes
and what you felt while you were following the imaginary circle.

Almost without exception, this first exercise produces a shape
which is very far removed from a circle! It is more like the battered
line in Fig.6a overleaf, and most people find the exercise difficult.

In the second part of the experiment, you and your partner sit
exactly as you did before. This time one partner aids the other by
tracing with their forefinger a perfect circle in the same place as
the imaginary one was. The partner who was not tracing the circle

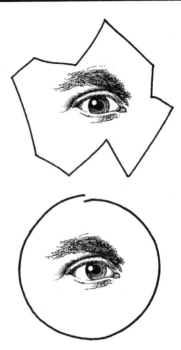

Fig. 6a Pattern showing unaided eye movement attempting to move around the circumference of a circle. *See page 59.*

Fig. 6b Pattern showing aided eye movement around the circumference of a circle. *See below.*

follows the tip of his partner's finger all round the circumference, noting how the eyes feel as they follow the fingertip. The partner who is guiding follows closely, as before, the eye movements of his partner. When this has been completed, reverse roles and then discuss what you noticed about your partner's eyes and your own.

During this exercise do not whip your finger around too quickly or in multiple circles, and do not try to hypnotize your partner!

Most partners find that, in this exercise, the eyes follow the guide smoothly, and are more comfortable doing so (see Fig. 6b above).

This is because the human eye is *designed* to follow movement, because it is movement in the environment that gives much survival information.

So, it seems that the child was correct in his actions, and so were you whenever you used a guide to assist you in any form of information-gathering. As this exercise demonstrates, eyes following a guide are much more relaxed and efficient.

WHAT'S THE BEST WAY TO USE A GUIDE?

As your eye is designed to follow a guide, as you probably used a guide as a child for your normal reading, and as you have also probably used a guide in different aspects of your reading throughout your life, it is very easy to re-learn this skill.

It is best to use a long thin object, such as a slim pen or pencil, a chopstick or a knitting needle. This way the guide does not block your view of the page because you can easily 'see around it'.

For this reason, it is not a particularly good idea to use your hand or finger, unless no other guide is available, because both the thickness of the fingers and the volume of the palm will block much of your vision.

To make the most effective use of the guide, simply place it underneath the line you are reading, and move it along smoothly as you read. Do not attempt to jerk it along in ideal fixation groups – your reading brain will instruct your eyes where to stop as you move the guide smoothly along the line.

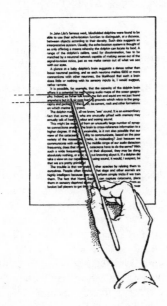

Fig. 7 Illustration showing the correct position for using the visual reading guide. *See page 62.*

An important question at this juncture is: do you need to move the guide along the entire line?

The answer to this question may be found in the common knowledge that speed readers read 'down the middle of the page'. This is often misinterpreted as meaning that their eyes go in a straight line down the centre. This is not the case. What they do is to read down the middle *section* of the page.

This is because the eyes can see up to five or six words at a time, so they can easily fixate after the beginning and before the end of the line, thus taking in the information 'to the side' (see Fig.7 on previous page).

The guide therefore minimizes the amount of work the eyes have to do, keeps the brain focused, and gives you constant accelerations in reading speed while maintaining high comprehension.

It takes less than an hour to re-establish this mental habit. The Eye-Cue section at the end of this chapter gives suggestions for practice.

In the following Self Test, you can combine what you previously learnt about your eye movements with what you have just learnt about guiding your eyes. It is advisable to practise using the guide for two minutes on material you have already read in this book, and then to jump straight into the Self Test.

SELF TEST 3   Animal Intelligence

Part I   A Whale of a Communicator
by Mowgli

A Canadian scientist has found that killer whales speak a number of different languages in a number of different dialects. The differences between the dialects can be as small as those distinguishing regional dialects of any national language, or as large as those between the European and Asian languages.

Super-Intelligent Linguistic Club

This finding places the whales in a super-intellegent linguistic club among mammals – a club that includes humans, major primates, and harbour seals. (Current research suggests that sounds produced by other mammals are determined genetically, although there is a growing band of researchers who consider that most animals are far more linguistically intelligent than we have previously assumed, and are species-wide and individually creative in their communication.)

John Ford, Curator of Marine Mammals at the Vancouver Public Aquarium in British Columbia, has been studying communications between killer whales for a decade. He observes that killer whale dialects are made up of the whistles and calls the animals use when communicating under water. These calls are quite distinct from the high-energy, sonar-like 'clicks' that the whales emit when navigating by echo-location.

Killer whales are actually members of the dolphin family, and are the largest in the family. Their name is a misnomer, there being no record that one has ever attacked a human – on the contrary there are a number of records that these whales, like dolphins, have often helped humans.

Whistling Whales

Perhaps a movement should be started to have them renamed – the 'Whistler Whale' or 'Whistling Whales' would be more appropriate, apart from being more onomatopoeic.

Whistling Whales are found in all the major oceans of the world, from the warmest, in the tropics, to the coldest in the Arctic and Antarctic. The largest concentrations are found off the coast of the cool countries, including Iceland and Canada.

The population Ford studied numbered approximately 350 who live for the entire year off the coast of British Columbia and northern Washington State in America. The whales have formed two separate communities which roam through adjacent territories.

The 'northern community' which consists of 16 family groups, or 'pods', ranges from mid-Vancouver Island to the south-eastern tip of Alaska. The members of the smaller 'southern community' divide themselves into three pods and wander from the border of the northern community all the way south into Puget Sound and Gary's Harbour.

Fortunately, most sounds produced by Whistling Whales are within the range of human hearing. Ford's research is therefore easy to carry out – he simply dangles a hydrophone over the side of the boat, and amplifies the sounds electronically, recording them on a tape recorder.

Through his research Ford has been able to identify the dialect of each pod. He has found that, on average, a pod makes 12 discrete calls. Each member of the pod is able to, and does, produce the full set of whistles and calls. The system of these whistles and calls is different, both quantitatively and qualitatively, from those of other dolphins and whales.

Most calls are used only within a pod, but sometimes one or more are common between pods.

Common Ancestors

Interestingly, Ford has found that these dialects are passed from generation to generation within each pod, leading him to speculate that groups which share calls are probably descended from a common ancestor or ancestors. The more calls two pods have in common, the closer the family relationship.

This phylo-genetic link between dialect and pod has enabled Ford to estimate how long it takes for a separate dialect to emerge. 'The rate of change appears to be very slow,' he says. 'It [a dialect] must require centuries to develop,' the implication being that some dialects could be thousands of years old.

One new focus of Ford's research has been the correlation between the behaviour of Whistling Whales and the calls they make.

So far he has not found a great correlation, although he has found that calls are faster, high in pitch, and more frequent when an animal is excited.

Ford currently believes that, taken together, the calls form an 'elaborate code of pod identity' which enables Whistler Whales to identify fellow members of their pod. This is especially important for keeping 'the family' together when collections of pods, known as 'super-pods', swim together.

So far, Ford has not been able to identify a grammatical structure in Whistler Whale communication. But he is impressed by its acoustic sophistication: 'They seem to have a very highly developed, efficient way of communicating that is something we can only partly understand at this point,' he says. 'I think, as time goes on, we will get a much better appreciation of just how remarkably adapted whales are to their unique environment.'

Part 2   Animal Intelligence – Dolphins
by Professor Michael Crawford and Mowgli

In terms of Rudyard Kipling's definition of learning as 'what, why, when, where and who', many people feel that the cetaceans (the whale family) are 'three serving men short' because there is 'no evidence' that they can communicate on matters of when, how and why. Some years ago I was duty officer at Whipsnade Zoo when an unscheduled performance was executed by the dolphins.

One out of three bottle-nosed dolphins *(Tursiops truncatus)* appeared to be sickly and an attempt was made to catch her. The response was that her two colleagues closed in and swam in tight formation on either side of her, preventing the placing of the net.

The solution was to chase them into the small side pool and bring down the separating sluice-gate to make the business easier. The dolphins' response was one of great agitation, which subsided when they lined up again in formation and dived to the bottom of the pool. In unison, they squeezed their noses under the bottom of the sluice-gate, flicked it up and swam to freedom.

That rather suggests they were capable of dealing with 'how' and 'when' and, at the start, had certainly come to a conclusion about 'why'.

It is consequently somewhat senseless to try to compare the brain function of *Homo sapiens* with *Tursiops truncatus* without properly defining the ground rules. A comparison of 'function' might be a more appropriate approach than 'intelligence'. Different species have different sets of problems and therefore there are different computer designs to deal with them. Some computers, like the LISP machine, are very clever at handling ideas, whereas others are better at handling numbers. Indeed it would be rather fruitless trying to compare a LISP with a BASIC program.

This high degree of cerebellar development in the dolphin family is likely to be related to the fact that the animal operates in a three-dimensional manner. Like the birds, it has a requirement for co-ordination in three dimensions which the cerebellum serves.

In John Lily's famous work, blindfolded dolphins were found to be able to use their echo-location function to distinguish, at a distance, between objects according to their density. Such data suggests an interpretative system. Usually, the echo-location system is thought of as only offering a means whereby the dolphin can locate its food. A range of the dolphin's calibre, used for discrimination, has to be matched by a neuronal network capable of making sense out of the signal-to-noise ratios, just as we make sense out of what we see with our eyes.

A glance at a baby dolphin's brain suggests a dense rather than loose neuronal packing, and as each neurone makes 6000 or more connections with other neurones, the likelihood that such a brain does little or nothing with its sensory inputs is, I would suggest, rather remote.

It is possible, for example, that the capacity of the dolphin brain offers it a potential for memorizing audio maps of the ocean geography. Indeed, as fisher folk know, the fish and squid are not just found anywhere but in their own feeding grounds which relate to the geography and geology of the ocean, its current, rock and other formations on which marine life grows.

The dolphin may, for all we know, 'see' sound. It is an extraordinary fact that some people who are unusually gifted with memory may actually talk of hearing colour and seeing sound.

This might be expected from an unusually large number of synaptic connections enabling the brain to cross-reference information to a higher degree. If that is conceivable, is it not also possible that our view of the cetaceans' inability to communicate, based on the poor variety of the noises they make, is misleading? Just because we communicate with words in the middle range of our audio detection frequency, does that mean the cetaceans have to do the same? With such a wide frequency range at their disposal, they may be doing absolutely nothing, or a lot, without knowing about it. If a dolphin did take a view on our capabilities in using sound, it would, I suspect, be that we are pretty primitive!

The trouble is that we analyse other species by relating them to ourselves. People often conclude that dogs and other animals are highly intelligent because they can perform simple tricks if we train them. The fact that *Homo sapiens* can capture cetaceans, place them in sensory-deprived environments and make them perform as basket ball players to get their food, simply demonstrates the power of such techniques.

Reducing the vast intelligence of these magnificent animals to mere party tricks is a minimalist, demeaning and ultimately unrewarding approach.

We would display our own intelligence and humanity more adequately by examining the vast range of abilities of our fellow creatures more humanely and intelligently.

* *

Stop Your Timer Now
Length of time: ....mins

Next calculate your reading speed in words per minute (wpm) by simply dividing the number of words in the passage (in this case 1601) by the time (in minutes) you took.

Speed Reading Formula:

$$\text{words per minute (wpm)} = \frac{\text{number of words}}{\text{time}}$$

When you have completed your calculation, enter the number in the wpm slot at the end of this paragraph, and enter it on your Progress Chart and your Progress Graph on page 187.

Words per minute: ....

SELF TEST 3: COMPREHENSION

1 Killer whales:
(a) speak a number of different languages in a number of different dialects
(b) one language in many different dialects
(c) two different languages in a single dialect each
(d) the same language in a number of different dialects

2 Whales are in a different 'linguistic club' from that of humans, major primates and harbour seals.   True/False

3 Killer whale dialects are made up of the whistles and calls the animals use when:
(a) navigating by echo-location
(b) communicating under water
(c) making love
(d) warning of danger

4 Records show that killer whales have:
(a) occasionally attacked humans
(b) regularly attacked humans
(c) never attacked humans
(d) attacked but not killed humans

5 Whistling whales are found in:
(a) only warm oceans
(b) only cool oceans
(c) only in the Atlantic and Arctic Oceans
(d) all the major oceans of the world

6 A family group of whales is called a ....

7 Most sounds produced by Whistling Whales are:
(a) above the range of human hearing
(b) below the range of human hearing
(c) within the range of human hearing
(d) undetectable

8 An average family of whales makes how many discrete calls?
(a) 8
(b) 10
(c) 12
(d) 20

9 Whale dialects are:
(a) a false label
(b) passed from generation to generation
(c) different from generation to generation
(d) fundamentally all the same

10 Ford estimated that a dialect takes how long to develop?
(a) a year
(b) 10 years
(c) a generation
(d) centuries

11 John Ford, by studying the 'acoustic sophistication' of the Whistling Whale, has at last identified the basic grammatical structure in their communication.   True/False

12 The high degree of cerebellar development in the dolphin family is likely to be related to the fact that:
(a) it needs a large brain to communicate
(b) it operates in a three-dimensional manner
(c) its oceanic environment allows for greater brain size
(d) it has had many more centuries than human beings to evolve

13 In John Lily's famous book, blindfolded dolphins were found to be able to use their echo-location function to distinguish, at a distance, between objects according to their:
(a) shape
(b) texture
(c) density
(d) colour

14 A glance at a baby dolphin's brain suggests a loose neuronal packing.   True/False

15 The dolphin's brain may:
(a) hear colours
(b) taste sound
(c) see sound
(d) taste colour

Check your answers against those on page 185.
Then divide your score by 15 and multiply by 100 to
calculate your percentage comprehension.

Comprehension score: .... out of 15
.... per cent

Now enter your score on your Progress Chart and your Progress Graph on page 187.

SUMMARY
1 The natural instinct of the child to use a guide when reading is correct.
2 The best guides are slim pens or pencils, knitting needles or even chopsticks.
3 The guide should move *smoothly* underneath the lines.
4 You need guide your eyes only down the *middle section* of the page.
5 The guide increases speed, improves concentration and comprehension and relaxes the eyes.

HIGH EYE-CUE ACTION POINTS
1 Use the best guide available to you at the moment, while at the same time searching for an ideal one.
2 Immediately re-read this chapter quickly, using a guide to do so.
3 Use a guide on the next newspaper and magazine that you read.
4 Occasionally 'push yourself' with the guide, reading a little bit too fast for comfort. This will gradually strengthen the 'muscle' of your speed and comprehension, in the same way that gradually increasing weights in the gym increases your physical muscular strength.

ONWORD
You have now graduated from the lower echelons of normal fast readers to the first rungs of the speed readers' ladder.

In the next chapter we break more boundaries by showing you the advanced uses of the guide and taking you into the realms of the super-speed reader.

CHAPTER SEVEN

Onward to Super-Speed Reading – The Speed Reading Hall of Fame

Great artists, thinkers, scientists and even some Presidents read at speeds of over 1000 words per minute. So can you.

FOREWORD

Chapter 7 introduces you to some of **the great speed readers of history** and **their speed reading feats**, explains how to **expand your side or peripheral vision**, and reveals **the secrets behind 'brain reading'**.

THE SPEED READING GREATS

The Speed Reading Hall of Fame

The Speed Reading Hall of Fame reads like a who's who of the great political, scientific and philosophic thinkers of all time – an indication that speed reading combined with the ability to understand, recall and use the material you read, plays a major role in achieving success.

John Stuart Mill

John Stuart Mill, the British utilitarian philosopher, ranked number 90 in the all-time list of great geniuses, is said to have read books by taking in entire pages in 'one visual gulp'.

Mill's story shows the importance of encouragement and motivation. In his early years, his father, a college professor, would give the young boy a book, tell him to go into another room for a brief period of time, read the book and then come back and discuss what he had absorbed.

This positive and high pressure on the young boy to concentrate and speed through the assigned material encouraged him to develop into an extremely competent speed reader.

One good way of increasing your own motivation and skill is to undertake the same exercise John Stuart Mill's father gave to him. You can discuss what you have absorbed with a friend or partner.

President Franklin D. Roosevelt

Franklin D. Roosevelt was one of the fastest and most voracious readers of the leaders of nations. It is reported that he could read an entire paragraph at a single glance, regularly completing a book at one sitting.

He apparently started out with average reading speeds, which he decided to work at improving. His first steps included increasing his original fixation span to four words per stop, then to six and eight words in a single fixation.

Roosevelt subsequently practised reading two lines at a time and then began to zig-zag his way down the pages, reading small paragraphs with single eye movements. His approach was identical to that of today's leading speed readers.

Professor C. Lowell Lees

Professor Lees was Chairman of the Speech Department at the University of Utah in the 1950s. Without him knowing it, his reading speed inspired one of the major advances in this field.

A young student, Evelyn Wood, handed in her 80-page term paper to the professor, expecting him to read it at his leisure and return it to her later.

To her surprise, he took the paper from her, completed it in under ten minutes, graded it and handed it back to her, as she sat in stunned amazement. Evelyn, who was later to become one of the leading figures in the Dynamic Reading movement, reported that Professor Lees *really had* read her paper. In the ensuing conversation, she found that he was not only completely familiar with everything she had written, including all her arguments; he was also aware of all the flaws in her work!

Assuming there were between 200 and 250 words per page, Professor Lees had read and fully comprehended her paper at a speed of approximately 2500 words per minute.

Inspired by this Evelyn Wood, researched the field thoroughly, and later went on to teach reading at the University of Utah and establish her own Dynamic Reading Institute.

President John F. Kennedy

President John F. Kennedy is perhaps the most famous speed reader ever. This is because he emphasized his intelligence and mental capacity during his campaigns, and made it publicly known that,having been a normal reader whose speed was approximately 284 words per minute, he had studied speed reading.

It became widely known that he worked at the skill until he had reached speeds of over 1000 words per minute. He also developed the ability to read at a great range of speeds, allowing him exceptional flexibility to vary his rate on the very different kinds of material he was obliged to read every day.

Sean Adam

Sean Adam, current world speed reading record holder, like many others, started as an average reader.

Sean's story is even more remarkable in that, as a child, he had serious visual problems, and spent years studying his visual system in order to improve his general eyesight which he did with remarkable persistence and dedication.

Once his eyes were working more flexibily Sean started, in 1982, to accelerate his reading speed, and currently holds the world record at a superb 3850 words per minute. Reports from his Alpha-Learning Institute in Europe indicate that he is preparing to take on all challengers, and has already stretched his own limits to a remarkable 4550 words per minute.

Vanda North

Vanda North, currently ranked third in the world, became interested in speed reading when she was President of the International Society for Accelerated Learning. What better activity for the President of such an organization than to accelerate her reading speed?

This Vanda did by practising all the techniques described in this book. In a very short time she was able to reach a comfortable 3000 words per minute. A particularly interesting point raised by Vanda is that, for years, she had been reading at a speed which, because it was 'normal', she assumed to be natural and unchangeable. When she realized the possibility of increasing her speed her initial reaction was one of extreme excitement. She set about reducing back-skipping and regression, increasing the speed of her eye movements and expanding the length of her fixations.

After seven minutes she had doubled her speed from 200 words per minute to 400! Her own reaction to this rapid improvement was one that surprises her to this day, for mixed with her elation was a deep fury. Vanda suddenly realized that for 21 years she could have been reading twice the amount, with *better* comprehension, or she could have read exactly the same amount and had nearly a year extra to be with friends, to travel, to explore and to have even more fun!

Vanda has also found that, contrary to all expectations, she is able to proofread material at five or ten times the rate of the average proofreader while making fewer errors. Practise your own super-speed reading techniques, and catch her if you can ... In fact, Vanda is the External Editor-in-Chief of the book you are now reading!

TWO FANTASTIC SPEED READING STORIES

Antonio di Marco Magliabechi

Antonio di Marco Magliabechi was a contemporary of Spinoza, Sir

Christopher Wren, Sir Isaac Newton and Leibniz. He was born on 29 October 1633 in Leonardo da Vinci's birthplace, Florence. His parents were so poor that they were unable to provide him with any formal education, and at a young age he was apprenticed to a local fruit dealer. Magliabechi spent his spare time in the shop trying to decipher what was on the pamphlets and journals that were used to wrap the groceries.

One of the shop's regular customers was a local bookseller who noted the young man's attempts to read the strange hieroglyphics before him. The bookseller took him to his own shop and Magliabechi was almost immediately able to recognize, remember and identify all the books. With the bookseller's help, Magliabechi eventually learnt to read properly and began to combine his new-found reading ability with phenomenal memorizing techniques which enabled him to remember nearly everything he read in its entirety (including punctuation).

A sceptical author decided to put the lad's growing reputation for speed reading and memory to the test and gave Magliabechi a new manuscript that he could never have seen before, telling him to read it for pleasure. Magliabechi duly read the manuscript at a remarkable speed and returned it almost immediately, confirming that he had read it in its entirety. A little while after the event, the author pretended that he had lost his manuscript and asked Magliabechi if he could help him to remember some of it. To his astonishment, the young man wrote out the entire book for him, transcribing perfectly every single word and every punctuation mark as if he had been copying from the original.

As time went on, Magliabechi read at greater and greater speeds and memorized increasingly large numbers of books. He eventually became so famous for the speed at which he devoured and absorbed knowledge that experts in all subjects came to him for instruction and source material in their own areas of interest. Whenever he was asked questions he answered by quoting verbatim from the books he had read and automatically memorized.

His reputation spread, and he was eventually hired by the Grand Duke of Tuscany to act as his personal librarian. In order to be able to handle the volume of material in the entire library, Magliabechi decided to develop his speed reading abilities to an almost superhuman extent. Contemporaries reported that he could simply 'dip' into a page, apparently absorbing the contents in their entirety with only one or two visual fixations, much to the amazement of those whom he allowed to watch him. He developed a reputation for having read and memorized the entire library!

Like most geniuses, Magliabechi continued to develop his abilities as he became older. The more he read and memorized, the faster he was able to read and the more he was able to remember. The story goes that, in his later years, he would lie in bed surrounded by volumes, each of which he would devour in less than half an hour, memorizing them in turn until he fell asleep. This he continued to do until his death in 1714 at the age of 81

If Magliabechi's eye/brain system was capable of such incredible reading and memory accomplishments, why do the rest of us crawl along at speeds which make us functionally illiterate by comparison? The answer appears to lie not in any lack of basic ability, but in the fact that we have actively and unwittingly trained ourselves to become slow. In other words, we have adopted belief systems, reading practices and habits that destroy our ability to read at any speed and with any reasonable comprehension.

Eugenia Alexeyenko
In his book *How to Pass Exams*, World Memory Champion and Grand Master of Memory Dominic O'Brien reports the incredible story of Eugenia whose accomplishments today seem to match those of Magliabechi 350 years ago.

According to a senior researcher at the Moscow Academy of Science, 'this amazing girl can read infinitely faster than her fingers can flick the pages – and if she didn't have to slow herself down by doing this, she would read at the rate of 416,250 words per minute'.

At the Kiev Brain Development Centre, a special test was set up for 18-year-old Eugenia, with a panel of scientists present. They were confident that the young girl had never read the test material before, because they had obtained copies of political and literary magazines that appeared on the news-stands that very day while Eugenia remained isolated in a room at the testing centre.

To make her task even more difficult, they obtained obscure and ancient books, as well as recently published ones from Germany which had been translated into Russian, the only language Eugenia knows.

While Eugenia was kept isolated and entertained, the examiners read the test materials several times and took copious notes on their contents. They then placed two pages of the material before her to see how fast she could read it.

The result was as stunning to them as Dr Lees' had been to Evelyn Wood and as Antonio Magliabechi's had been to his contemporaries. Eugenia apparently read 1390 words in a fifth of a second – the time it takes to blink your eyes. Eugenia was also given several magazines, novels and reviews which she also read effortlessly.

One of the examiners reported: 'We quizzed her in detail and often it was very technical information that a normal teenager would never have been able to understand. Yet she gave answers that proved that she understood perfectly.'

Remarkably, no one knew of the young girl's unique ability until she was 15 years old. At that time her father, Nikolai, gave her a copy of a long newspaper article. When she handed it back to him two seconds later, saying she found it interesting, he assumed she was joking. When he questioned her on the content, however, all her answers were correct.

Eugenia herself says: 'I don't know what my secret is. The pages go into my mind and I recall the "sense" rather than the exact text. There is some sort of analysis going on in my brain which I really can't explain. But I feel as if I have a whole library in my head!'

EXPANDING YOUR VISUAL POWER

In Chapter 6 you discovered that your eye was capable of taking in more words per horizontal fixation. You are now going to do a series of exercises which will prove that your perceptual abilities stretch far beyond even your current improved capability (see Fig. 8, overleaf).

Measuring Your Horizontal and Vertical Vision

First, looking straight into the distance and keeping your focus on a point as far away as possible, touch the tips of your two forefingers together, horizontally in front of you, 75 cm (3 inches) from the bridge of your nose. Begin wriggling the tips of your forefingers, and slowly pull them apart along a horizontal line, keeping your eyes focused in the distance. Only when you can no longer see the movement of the tips of your fingers out of the 'corners of your eyes', do you stop, and measure the distance of your **horizontal vision**.

In the second part of the exercise, do exactly the same, this time placing the tips of your fingers vertically, and again wriggling them and slowly pulling the fingers apart until you can no longer see the movement out of the top and bottom of your field of vision. Only now do you stop, and measure the distance of your **vertical vision**. Do these exercises **now**.

The Results

Amazing, wasn't it! People often find that their horizontal vision is as far as their arms can stretch. The vertical vision is slightly shorter but only because of the eyebrow bone.

How is this possible?

The answer lies in the way the human eye is designed. Each of your eyes has 130 million light receivers in its retina, which means that you have 260 million receivers of light in total.

What percentage of your eyes do you think is devoted to your 'clear' or central focus and what percentage is devoted to your 'side' or peripheral focus? Fill in your answers opposite:

Percentage
Central focus: ....
Side focus: ....

In fact, your clear focus has only 20 per cent of the eye/brain system devoted to it, while your peripheral focus has a staggering 80 per cent! This means that, of the 260 million light receivers you have working for you, over 208 million are devoted to your peripheral vision.

Why is such a large percentage devoted to this? The reason is that most of the events in the universe are happening *around* your central focus, and it is essential for your survival that your brain be aware of every change in your environment in order to direct you *towards* what you need, and *away* from danger.

In traditional methods of teaching reading we have concentrated only on the clear focus vision, thus using less than 20 per cent of the visual capacity available to us, and using even that small percentage in an utterly inappropriate way.

Readers like Antonio Magliabechi, John Stuart Mill and President Kennedy all trained themselves to utilize the vast untapped potential of their peripheral vision. You can do the same.

Seeing with Your Mind's Eye
You are about to perform an experiment in perception that will astonish you and will change you for life. What you will be doing in this experiment is disconnecting your brain from your clear focus, and actively seeing with your *Mind's Eye*.

When you have read this paragraph, turn to page 77, and place your finger directly underneath the word 'lines' in the middle of the page. Keeping your eye totally focused on that central word:

1 See how many words you can see to either side of the central word without moving your eyes.
2 See how many words you can see clearly above and below the word you are pointing at.
3 See if you can tell whether there is a number at the top or bottom of the page and, if so, what it is.
4 See if you can count the number of paragraphs on the page.
5 See if you can count the number of paragraphs on the opposite page.
6 Can you see if there is a diagram on either of the pages?
7 If you can see the diagram or illustration, can you clearly or roughly determine what it is?

Do this exercise *now*.

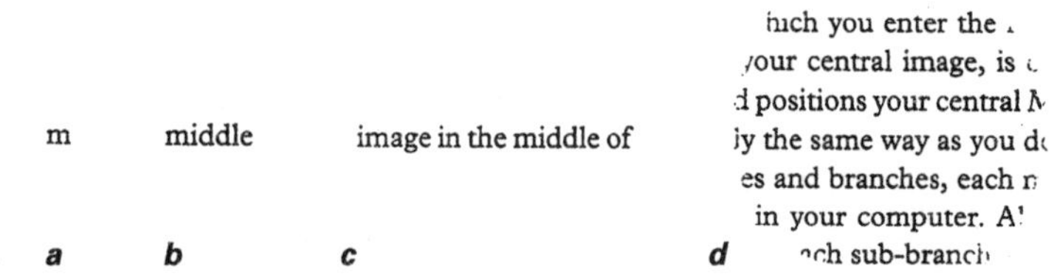

m   middle   image in the middle of

a   *b*   *c*   *d*

Fig. 8 Development of increased visual field in advanced readers. *a* Focus on a single letter, as when a child first learns to read by the phonic method. *b* Focus on a single word (the poor-to-average reader). *c* Focus on 45 words at a time (the good reader). *d* Focus on groups or bunches of words (the advanced reader).

The Results
Most people answer 'yes' to most of the questions. This easy exercise demonstrates that your brain acts as a giant central eye that scans the entire world behind the lenses of your physical eyes.

Whereas most people spend their lives with their brains shackled to the 'tunnel vision' of direct focus, the better readers, thinkers and survivors use the full range of their brains' visual skills.

Cyclopean Perception
Your brain's ability to see with its central eye recently exploded into the popular arena with the *Magic Eye* series of books. These books were based on the ground-breaking work of Professor Bela Julesz of the Sensory and Perceptual Process Department of Bell Telephone Laboratories.

Julesz's images are composed of two sets of finely woven dots. Each set forms part of an image. Each eye takes in a part, seeing only a flat representation. Your staggeringly sophisticated brain performs an astonishingly complex mathematical and geometric feat, combining both images to give dramatic three-dimensional pictures that are seen not in external reality, but only by the brain (see Plate III).

BRAIN READING
The revolutionary new approach being offered to you in *The Speed Reading Book* is that, from now on, you will read with your brain as the central focus of your attention, and not your eyes. Your eyes are a million-faceted puppet; your brain the master puppeteer.

The super-speed reader of the future will be the person who combines peripheral vision with cyclopean perception (see Fig.9, opposite) to take in, as Magliabechi did, entire paragraphs and pages at a time – an accomplishment which, in the light of our new aware-ness, now seems far more attainable. One easy way to do this is to

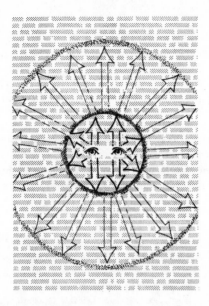

Fig. 9 Fields of vision. The inner circled area shows the area of clear vision available to the speed reader when the eye/brain system is used properly. The outer circle shows the peripheral vision *also* available.

develop your fledgling skill with the guide into more advanced meta-guiding techniques (see Chapter 8).

In addition to using meta-guiding techniques, you can also expand the use of your peripheral and cyclopean perception by holding the book at a greater distance from your eyes than normal. By doing so, you allow your peripheral vision to see the page far more clearly as you read.

The tremendous advantage of this is that, while your clear focus is reading the one, two or three lines on which you are concentrating, your 'brain reader' is using its peripheral vision to review what you have already read and preview the text to come. In this way it is vastly improving your memory of the material you have already covered, and is also preparing you for the material ahead, much as a reconnaissance scout prepares troops for safer and more speedy movement across unknown territory.

An added advantage of this 'soft focus' approach is that your eyes have to do far less tight muscular fixating. They therefore become far less tired and you feel able to go on reading for longer periods of time. Many people find that, by using this approach, stiff necks and headaches (a common problem for many readers) are eliminated.

SUMMARY

1 Speeds of over 1000 words per minute are definitely attainable – many historical figures have accomplished these and higher speeds with ease.

2 Your eyes contain 260 million light receivers.

3 More than 80 per cent of these light receivers are devoted to your peripheral vision.

4 Your peripheral vision is exceptionally wide and very deep.

5 It is your brain that reads – your eyes are simply the very sophisticated lenses it uses.

6 The super-speed readers of the future will be 'brain readers', using both the full range of their peripheral vision and their cyclopean perception.

HIGH EYE-CUE ACTION POINTS

1 In your daily life, set yourself brain perception goals. Start by getting your brain's eye to hunt out a particular set of objects or colours or shapes in your environment.

2 Try using your brain's eye when you read *anything*.

3 Continue practising with your guide, occasionally experimenting with taking two lines at a time.

4 Always have your reading material as far away from your eyes as you can comfortably manage.

ONWORD

You have now made the leap from being a normal speed reader (focusing primarily on your eyes) to being a super-speed reader (focusing primarily on your brain). In the next chapter you will be introduced to some meta-guiding techniques which together harness your peripheral vision and your cyclopean perception.

CHAPTER EIGHT

Meta-Guiding Towards 'Photographic Memory' Reading Levels

The photographic imaging capacity of the human eye is thousands of times more sophisticated than the most advanced cameras. The full range of its ability has yet to be explored.

FOREWORD

This chapter provides you with **nine major practical guiding techniques** to help you strengthen and gain control of your peripheral vision and your cyclopean perception.

YOUR PHOTOGRAPHIC MEMORY CAPACITY

Open this book at any page, and glance at the page for one second – can you remember any word, graph, shape or sentence? Would you recognize the page again? As we now know, we *do* take the information in. If you doubt the truth of this, think of what your eyes immediately take in when you suddenly drive round a bend on a mountain road: many cars and lorries coming towards you, many going in the same direction as you; tens of millions of trees, thousands of houses and possibly birds and animals as well. All this is done in a fraction of a second! Think how tiny, by comparison, a mere few words on a page is – you *can* do it!

The skills you are about to learn will introduce you to the advanced use of the visual guide, and will enable you to experiment with accelerated reading movements that take into account your vertical as well as your horizontal peripheral vision.

META-GUIDING – THE TECHNIQUES

The meta-guiding techniques that follow use your peripheral vision, your cyclopean eye, and the astonishingly quick photographic ability of your eye/brain system.

It is especially useful to practise all of them initially at very high speeds, aiming for virtually no comprehension, and then to practise them immediately at your new normal speeds. In this way your brain will become accustomed to high speeds. It is often best to begin by using these techniques on material you have already read – thus accomplishing two tasks at once: reviewing what you have read while 'warming up' your eye/brain system for the task ahead. When

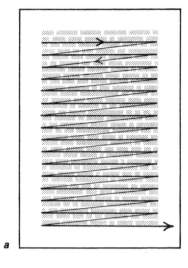

a

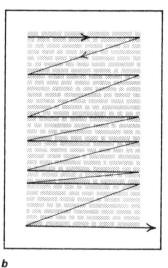

b

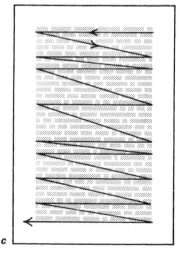

c

Fig. 10
Meta-guiding techniques.
See opposite.
a The double line sweep
b The variable sweep
c The reverse sweep.

you have completed this chapter, practise all the meta-guiding techniques on everything you have read so far. As you do so, try to practise at speeds that push you to the limit.

The Double Line Sweep
The double line sweep (see Fig.10a, opposite) is identical to the original technique you used for guiding your eyes, the only difference being that you consistently take in two lines at a time.

To perform this exercise correctly, move your guide smoothly and gently along underneath two lines, lifting the guide a fraction of a centimetre off the page on the return sweep, then moving it again smoothly underneath the next two lines. The double line sweep is an excellent way of getting your brain accustomed to using its vertical vision as well as its horizontal vision. This is much easier than you might expect, and many cultures use vertical as their *primary* vision. For example, the Japanese and Chinese have favoured vertical over horizontal for thousands of years.

Similarly, musicians, as a matter of necessity, combine vertical with horizontal vision when reading music. If you can read music, you should be able to transfer the skill you have already acquired to double-line sweep reading.

The Variable Sweep
The variable sweep (see Fig.10b, opposite) is identical to the double line sweep, except that it allows you to take in as many lines as you feel you can at a time. Advanced speed readers usually take in between two and eight lines with each sweep.

'Backward' Reading – The Reverse Sweep
'Backward' reading (see Fig.10c, opposite) has the advantage of allowing you to instantaneously double your reading speed by using the backward sweep of your eyes to *take in* information rather than simply get you back to the beginning of the next line.

'What?' you say. 'Don't be ridiculous – reading backwards would simply leave a jumble of meaningless words in my head.'

Reading backwards is easier than you might think. After all, many cultures prefer reading from right to left, notably the Arabic and Israeli.

That is not all, however. The secret of reading backwards lies in the fact that in reality you are *not* reading backwards! If you take in five or six words per fixation, which by now you should comfortably be doing, what you see in each fixation is in the correct order. Therefore reading backwards is fundamentally the same as normal reading. The only additional work your brain has to do is to put large chunks of meaning in order, much like a jigsaw puzzle. Your brain always does this when reading anyway, as, for example, in the following sentence: 'People who believe that normal reading speeds of above 1000 words per minute are possible are correct.' In this example your brain had to hold everything 'in waiting' until it received the final piece of information which made all the others make sense. In backward reading the process is identical. You will find it surprisingly easy and rewarding.

The reverse sweep uses exactly the same hand motions as the double line sweep and the variable sweep, simply reversing the technique (see page 80).

Advanced Visual Guiding Movements
The 'S', the zig-zag, the loop, the vertical wave and the lazy 'S' can all be done at different speeds and at different angles.

For in-depth reading, as much as 30 seconds per page may be required. For training, surveying, previewing and reviewing, ten seconds per page should be the maximum.

The double margins technique, in which either a finger or a thumb goes down the left margin, and your visual guide down the right-hand margin, is useful primarily for study reading, and can be varied by making either the left or right visual guide movement into a vertical wave.

The 'S'
The 'S' technique (see Fig.11a, opposite) combines the forward and reverse sweeps, and can be used as a single line sweep, a double line sweep or a variable sweep.

The Zig-Zag
The zig-zag (see Fig.11b, opposite) is a very advanced meta-guiding technique which makes particular use of the entire field of your peripheral vision.

In this technique you gently move your guide diagonally down a few lines, gently perform a little needle's-eye loop near the margin, then sweep back diagonally down the page, performing another little loop in the opposite margin, and so on, until you reach the bottom of the page.

This technique and the others can be horizontally lengthened or shortened, allowing you to move the guide all the way to the margins if you feel the need, or to condense it into the middle two-thirds of the page, allowing your horizontal peripheral vision to take in the information near the margins.

The Loop
The loop (see Fig.11c, opposite) is similar in style to the zig-zag, the only difference being that the little needle's eye becomes a large area of text that can itself be taken in with one soft-focus fixation.

The loop is an especially rhythmical technique, and is a favourite among advanced speed readers.

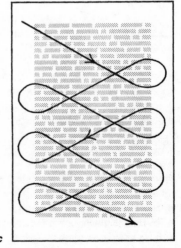

Fig. 11
Advanced visual
guiding movements.
See pages 82 and 85.
a The 'S'
b The zig-zag
c The loop.

83

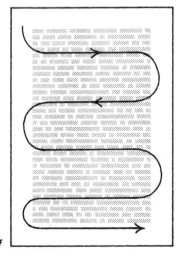

d

e

Fig. 11
Advanced visual guiding
movements, continued.
d The vertical wave
e The double guide
f The lazy 'S'.

f

The Vertical Wave

The vertical wave (see Fig.11d, opposite) is the technique that often leads the uninformed to believe that speed readers read 'down the middle of the page' in a straight line. In fact their eyes glide in rhythmical waves, moving slightly left and right, down the centre *section* of the page. The vertical wave is an ideal technique from this point of view because it combines 'forward' and 'backward' reading, also allowing the horizontal peripheral vision and the vertical peripheral vision to be used to their maximum extent.

The Double Guide

The double guide or double margin technique (see Fig.11e, opposite) involves using two guides, often a finger or thumb on one side, and your standard guide on the other, moving each in unison smoothly down the page margins, while your eyes devour the information in between.

This technique is excellent for allowing your brain to dictate where your eyes go. If you have already established your general goals for the reading, your cyclopean eye will search out the information. There is no need for you to force your eyes to fixate in particular areas. Your brain will take care of you.

The Lazy 'S'

The lazy 'S' (see Fig. 11f, opposite) combines elements of the basic 'S', the zig-zag and the vertical wave. In fact, it could be considered to be a larger version of each.

In this technique you simply sculpt a large series of normal and reverse 'S's' down the page, usually completing a page with five horizontal or slightly vertical movements.

PUTTING THESE META-GUIDING TECHNIQUES INTO PRACTICE

These techniques can be used for previewing, for skimming and scanning, for surveying, as exercises to increase your reading speed, as exercises to develop your peripheral vision, as a general 'work-out' for your eyes, and, as the best speed readers are finding, for normal reading.

One of the most dramatic stories involving the use of meta-guiding concerns a 35-year-old lady who was attending one of my speed reading courses, a course which consisted of eight three-hour lessons each spaced a week apart.

During the lesson when the meta-guiding techniques were being introduced, the class had to use the loop or the vertical wave or the lazy 'S' as a super-fast previewing technique on a novel. The time limit for completing the entire book was five minutes.

The lady in question left the class in frustration, saying that although she had used the guide on every page, not a single thing had gone in, and she 'couldn't see the point'.

During the following week's lesson, the same novel was used for an exercise in which the students had to use any guiding technique, and to read for good comprehension. The lady chose the basic 'S', and began, with the rest of the class, the 15-minute exercise. After five minutes the concentrated silence was broken by a shriek! The lady was screaming, 'I know it! I know it! I know it!'

She reported that, as she became accustomed to the guide, the book suddenly opened itself to her like a film that she had already seen once and was seeing for the second time.

What had happened was that her brain had photographed the entire book, storing it somewhere deep in her visual cortex and cyclopean mind's eye. When the brain was stimulated again it simply re-accessed the information and gave it to her.

In the Eye-Cue exercises at the end of this chapter, you will be given several practical and exciting methods for establishing these new reading techniques and for increasing your speed.

PERCEPTION EXERCISE 2
The number exercises that follow will help develop your awareness of both your vertical and horizontal vision. For this reason, each number group is on two lines. Uncover each block of two numbers and recover them, giving yourself enough time for only a short glance. Write what you think you saw on the line and check. When you have practised a few of these exercises, move on to Self Test 4 Before reading, select your favourite meta-guiding technique, raise your motivational levels, and go for your own personal speed reading record to date!

28	84
92	21 ....
94	14
07	68 ....
93	35
12	56 ....
86	48
74.....................	99 ....
06	18
93	10 ....
57	39
72.....................	51 ....
30	74
66	33 ....

73
16 ....

03
48 ....

71
95 ....

39
68 ....

96
04 ....

53
18 ....

08
42 ....

41
40 ....

39
15 ....

83
40 ....

56
14 ....

94
016 ....

18
964 ....

68
922 ....

46
921 ....

04
962 ....

49
763 ....

91
217 ....

84
28 ....

98
32 ....

39
18 ....

47
13 ....

70
15 ....

94
75 ....

29
65 ....

78
70 ....

73
31 ....

14
77 ....

93
36 ....

18
936 ....

93
148 ....

25
096 ....

84
695 ....

98
277 ....

77
194......................

04
185 ....

86	27
103	976 ....
93	60
184	414 ....
37	22
629	050 ....
94	32
060	281 ....
46	18
299	504 ....
37	95
276	706 ....
07	20
330	063 ....
13	30
966	411 ....
95	84
563	392 ....
52	78
380	153 ....
50	72
064	927 ....
11	63
693	832 ....
695	592
802	033 ....
938	153
805	408 ....
463	916
592	863 ....
907	106
818	763 ....
953	909
832	753 ....
711	063
393	494 ....

512	508
937	342 ....
830	174
148	673 ....
602	725
935	163 ....
291	408
175	853 ....
784	591
421	744 ....
594	422
208	906 ....
440	807
618	945 ....
128	705
483	912 ....
058	614
983	937 ....
163	731
975	147 ....
805	853
194	902 ....
254	395
110	707 ....

You are now ready for Self Test 4. While you are reading this Self Test, make sure you take in large groups of words with each 'visual gulp', use your guide to assist you, and hold the book a good distance away from you, thus enabling you to make use of your peripheral vision and your 'brain reading' capabilities.

SELF TEST 4   Are We Alone in the Universe? Extra-Terrestrial Intelligences
by Tony Buzan

Since 1960, at least 80 investigations have been carried out searching for intelligent life elsewhere in the universe. All of these have been on so small a scale that they were almost inevitably doomed to failure. Now NASA has started searching with new equipment that promises to be ten million times more effective than anything tried before.

With human and computer intelligence searching for extra-terrestrial intelligence on such a massively increasing scale, a number of scientists are predicting that it will be found before the turn of the century.

On precisely the day, hour and minute of the five hundredth anniversary of Columbus' discovery of America, the human race launched history's greatest-ever effort to discover not only new worlds but, more importantly, new intelligences.

On 12 October 1992, at 3 pm Atlantic Standard Time, astronomers in Arecibo, Puerto Rico, turned on the most powerful radio telescope ever built. At precisely the same moment, others fired up a second telescope at the Goldstone Tracking Station near Barstow, California. More than a hundred physicists, astronomers, computer programmers and technicians are now assiduously monitoring control panels in eager anticipation as super-computers listen to millions of radio channels, searching for any signal that bears the stamp of intelligent life, and which confirms what the majority of astronomers have believed for years – that we are not alone in the universe.

The 100-million dollar project, called SETI (Search for Extra-Terrestrial Intelligence) has full NASA mission status, and will continue until at least the year 2000, in the hope of discovering radio waves created by intelligent beings: radio waves that might have begun their journey towards Earth at the speed of light as recently as yesterday or perhaps as distantly as ten billion years ago.

The mission dwarfs our previous greatest attempt at searching for extra-terrestrial intelligence inspired by the astronomer Frank Drake in 1974. Drake used the Arecibo radio telescope, which at the time had an effective power of 20 trillion watts, to send a coded message towards the great cluster of stars in the constellation Hercules, some 24,000 light years away.

The message, a kind of cosmic IQ test, was shown first by Drake to the astronomer Carl Sagan, one of the finalists in last year's Brain of the Year award, over lunch at the Cornell Faculty Club. According to Drake, Sagan worked out most of it fairly quickly.

The message, from top to bottom, shows:

1 A binary counting system.
2 Molecules essential for life on Earth.
3 Chemical formulae for DNA, our genetic material.
4 A graphic representation of the double helix shape of the DNA molecule ending at the head of a human figure.
5 A representation of our sun and nine planets (Earth is raised to show where we live), and a depiction of a radio telescope beaming the message.

The current mission is so enormous in its scale and precise in its engineering that we will be able to hear more in three days than we have heard in the 22 years since Drake began his initial experiments in 1970 In the new effort, at least six radio telescopes worldwide will eventually go on constant alert; the dish at Arecibo – 03 km (1/5 mile) in diameter – has been upgraded to increase its sensitivity by 300 per cent and extraordinary software has been designed to interpret signals. Drake, 62, is Professor of Astronomy at the University of California, Santa Cruz, and is also President of the SETI Institute in Mountain View, California. He says, 'I find nothing more tantalizing than the thought that radio messages from alien civilizations in space are passing through our offices and homes right now, like a whisper we can't quite hear.'

The Eyes

The largest radio telescope in the world is very different from the traditional optical telescopes used by amateur astronomers, or even the huge tubular telescopes that peer out of observatory domes and mountains around the world, like Palomar California, or Mauna Kea in Hawaii. The Arecibo telescope is a 304 m (1000 foot) wide bowl of perforated aluminium set in a vast hole in the ground. Above the bowl, hundreds of tonnes of steerable antennae hang from cables that are connected to support towers on the surrounding hills.

Similar in design to a TV satellite dish, a radio telescope can focus every radio wave that hits it towards a central collection point where the signal is then fed to, and processed by, a receiver.

These 'eyes of the Earth' are so sensitive that, in 1987, a new super-computer connected to the Goldstone radio telescope in the Mojave Desert easily detected the faint, 1-watt signal emanating from the Pioneer 10 probe that was launched from Earth in the winter of 1972 At the time it was detected, Pioneer was 64 billion km (4 billion miles) out in space!

Radio telescopes are especially useful in the search for extra-terrestrial intelligence, because radio waves given off by stars are both irregular and random, while radio waves used for intelligent communication form patterns that are easily detected on display monitors such as oscilloscopes.

The idea of searching for non-random waves that would suggest the presence of intelligence originally formed in the mid-1950s in the minds of Drake and of physicists Guiseppe Cocconi and Philip Morrison at Cornell. In 1959, in the science journal *Nature*, Cocconi and Morrison wrote: '... the probability of success is difficult to estimate, but if we never search, the chance of success is zero.'

History's Biggest Bargain

To those who question whether the effort is worthwhile, Drake points out that the £135 million earmarked for SETI is less than one-tenth of 1 per cent of NASA's annual budget of £15 billion. 'When you factor in the consequences of success,' Drake says, 'this could be the biggest bargain in history.'

A large percentage of the budget goes on new computer equipment which both enhances the quality of reception and helps in the interpretation of signals.

These giant electronic brains will 'perceive' vast quantities of cosmic radio information which will be spread over millions of channels, and will sift through the data, culling patterns and possibilities for the human observers.

The brain behind these brains is extraordinary in its own right: physicist Kent Cullers has been blind since birth, and has never seen a radio signal on an oscilloscope, let alone a star. His passion for the universe stems from his father who, when Cullers was five, read to him from *The Golden Book of Astronomy*. 'The idea that there might be other worlds to discover fired my imagination,' he recalls. And his massive imagination is what is helping to give the Earth sight: he has managed to endow his automated signal processing programme with what *Life* magazine describes as 'second sight' – a system that can identify suspiciously intelligent signals in what would otherwise appear to be nothing more than a sound-cauldron of hissing static.

The head of the NASA project, Professor Jill Tarter believes (as do her colleagues) that other intelligent life does exist. She and her colleagues envision a galactic community of intelligent civilizations, too far apart to socialize, colonize or cannibalize one another. A message from any one of them, sent to Earth perhaps many millions of years ago when our civilization was not yet existent, could reach us at any time. And what if the project does 'unEarth' the signals for which they search? Tarter says: 'Any signals that arrive are rightly the property of humankind. They were sent to the planet Earth, not to NASA. After millennia of wondering, all humans should know – we are not alone.'

Human as Guardian

Arthur C. Clarke, Chancellor of the International Space University, and author of *2001 – A Space Odyssey*, believes the search has tremendous scientific and moral value.

In *Life* he writes:

However it might occur, the detection of intelligent life beyond the Earth would change forever our outlook on the universe. At the very least, it would prove that intelligence does have some survival value, despite what we see on the evening news.

SETI represents the highest possible form of exploration, and when we cease to explore, we will cease to be human.

But suppose the whole argument for SETI is flawed, and intelligent life has arisen only on Earth. It would, of course, be impossible to prove that – there might always be ET's just a few light years beyond our range of investigation. If, however, after centuries of listening and looking, we have found no sign of extra-terrestrial intelligence, we would be justified in assuming that we are.

'And that is the most awesome possibility of all. We are only now beginning to appreciate our duty towards the planet Earth: if we are indeed the sole heirs to the galaxy, we must also be its future guardians.'

After millions of years of living in isolation, human intelligence may be within a mere ten years of realizing that it has companions in the cosmos.

* *

Stop Your Timer Now
Length of time: .... mins

Next, calculate your reading speed in words per minute (wpm) by simply dividing the number of words in the passage (in this case 1495 words) by the time (in minutes) you took.

Speed Reading Formula:
words per minute (wpm) = $\dfrac{\text{number of words}}{\text{time}}$

When you have completed your calculation, enter the number in the wpm slot at the end of this paragraph, and enter it on your Progress Chart and your Progress Graph on page 187.

Words per minute: ....

SELF TEST 4: COMPREHENSION

1 Since 1960, at least how many investigations have been carried out searching for intelligent life elsewhere in the universe?
(a) 60
(b) 80
(c) 55
(d) 75

2 When did the human race launch history's greatest-ever effort to discover new intelligences?
(a) the hundredth anniversary of Columbus' discovery of America
(b) the fiftieth anniversary of the launch of the first satellite
(c) the five hundredth anniversary of Columbus' discovery of America
(d) on no particular historical day

3 SETI stands for Searching for Extra-Territorial Intellects.   True/False

4 NASA is searching for radio waves that might have begun their journey towards Earth at the speed of light as distantly as:
(a) a million years ago
(b) a hundred million years ago
(c) a billion years ago
(d) ten billion years ago

5 The previous greatest attempt at searching for extra-terrestrial beings in 1974 was inspired by:
(a) Frank Drake
(b) Carl Sagan
(c) President Kennedy
(d) Mensa

6 The 1974 attempt sent a coded message towards the great cluster of stars in the constellation known as:
(a) Jupiter
(b) Orion
(c) Hercules
(d) Scorpio

7 In that coded message was included a representation of our sun and nine planets.   True/False

8 In the new effort, at least how many radio telescopes worldwide will eventually be on constant alert?
(a) two
(b) four
(c) six
(d) eight

9 The Arecibo telescope is a wide bowl of perforated aluminium set in a vast hole in the ground. How wide is it?
(a) 304 m (100 feet)
(b) 152 m (500 feet)
(c) 228 m (750 feet)
(d) 304 m (1000 feet)

10 A radio telescope can focus towards a central collection point:
(a) 25 per cent of the radio waves that hit it
(b) 50 per cent of the radio waves that hit it
(c) 75 per cent of the radio waves that hit it
(d) all the radio waves that hit it

11 Radio waves given off by stars are:
(a) irregular and random
(b) irregular and not random

(c) not random and irregular
(d) not irregular and not random

12 The brain behind the brains of the SETI search is extraordinary because:
(a) he has the highest IQ in the world
(b) he was originally not interested in astronomy
(c) he has been blind since birth
(d) he was originally a doctor of medicine

13 Who has been described as giving the Earth sight?
(a) Frank Drake
(b) Kent Cullers
(c) Jill Tarter
(d) Galileo

14 Professor Jill Tarter hopes but does not believe that other intelligent life does exist. True/False

15 Arthur C. Clarke said, 'SETI represents the highest possible form of exploration, and when we cease to explore, we will cease to be ....'

Check your answers against those on page 185.
Then divide your score by 15 and multiply by 100 to
calculate your percentage comprehension.

Comprehension score: .... out of 15
.... per cent

Now enter your score on your Progress Chart and your Progress Graph on page 187.

SUMMARY
Using meta-guiding techniques greatly enhances the value of the visual guide. The main meta-guiding techniques are:

• The Double Line Sweep
• The Variable Sweep
• 'Backward' Reading – The Reverse Sweep
• The 'S'
• The Zig-Zag
• The Loop
• The Vertical Wave
• The Double Guide
• The Lazy 'S'

HIGH EYE-CUE ACTION POINTS

1 Practise with each of the meta-guiding techniques for at least five minutes, varying your speed and depth of comprehension as you go. The five minutes is necessary to allow your brain time to get used to the technique.

2 When you have done this, select your three favourite meta-guiding techniques and practise with them. In all these exercises, it is useful to practise on material you have already read, as this makes it much easier to get used to your new habit. Constantly reviewing *The Speed Reading Book* will help you both practise your new techniques and review essential information.

3 Give yourself a number of five-minute readings in which you start reading for comprehension using your favourite meta-guiding technique, and gradually increase your reading speed so that, by the end of the five minutes, you are getting 5 to 10 per cent comprehension. This exercise will allow you to 'pull yourself up by the boot straps' as your eyes become more and more accustomed to higher speeds.

4 Practise meta-guiding techniques at wildly varying speeds. Many people find, to their amazement, that at lower speeds their comprehension is almost absent, but at certain specific rhythms their comprehension suddenly becomes amazingly clear.

ONWORD
The meta-guiding techniques you have learnt in this chapter will be of particular help in acquiring the skills you are about to learn in Chapter 9 – Developing Your Advanced Skimming and Scanning Skills. By applying meta-guiding techniques you will at least double your speed in skimming and scanning.

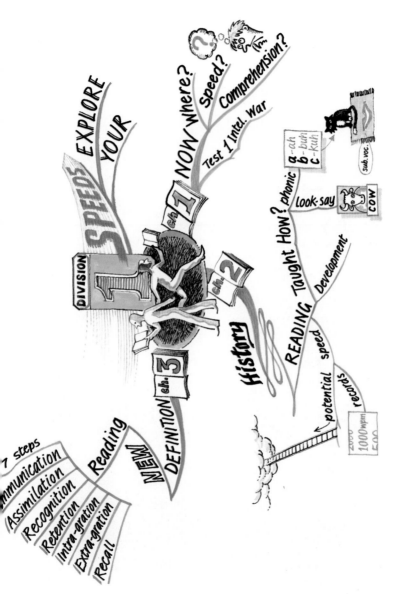

Plate I Mind Map of Division One

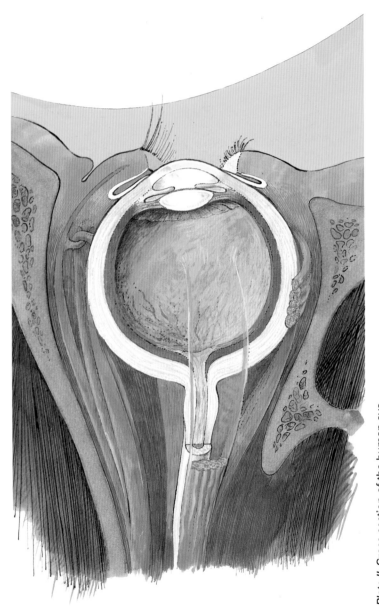

Plate II Cross-section of the human eye

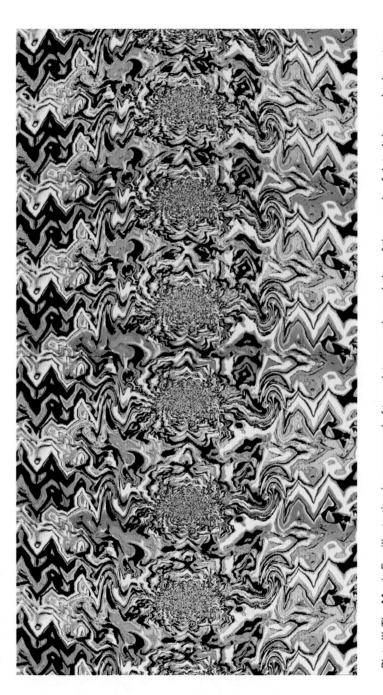

Plate III The Magic Eye illustration is composed of two pictures each consisting of thousands of dots. It is your *brain*, not your eyes, which fantastically combines these into a single clear image. *This* is the process *The Speed Reading Book* teaches you how to use to become a super-speed reader. A clue to help you 'see' this image is that it relates perfectly to this book.

Plate IV Mind Map of Division Two

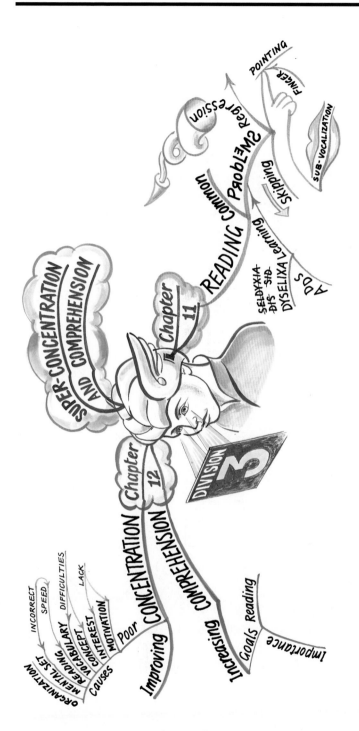

Plate V Mind Map of Division Three

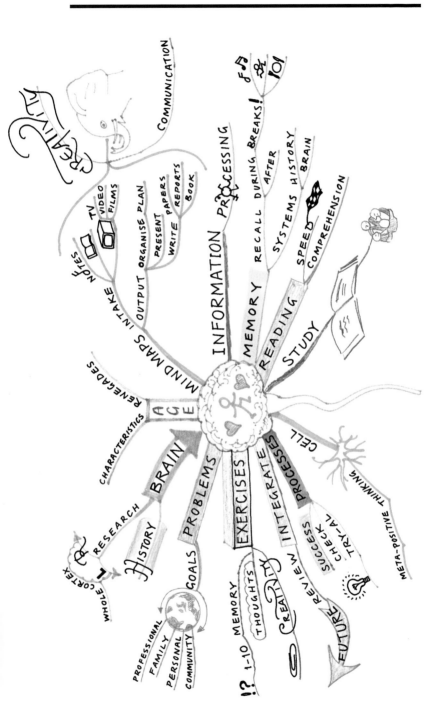

Plate VI Mind Map by a company director

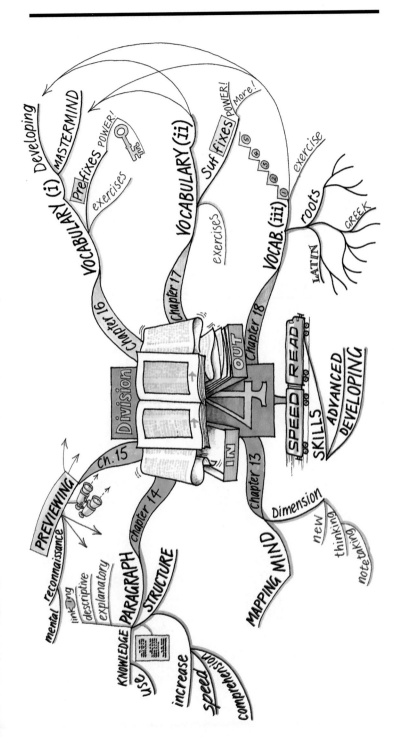

Plate VII Mind Map of Division Four

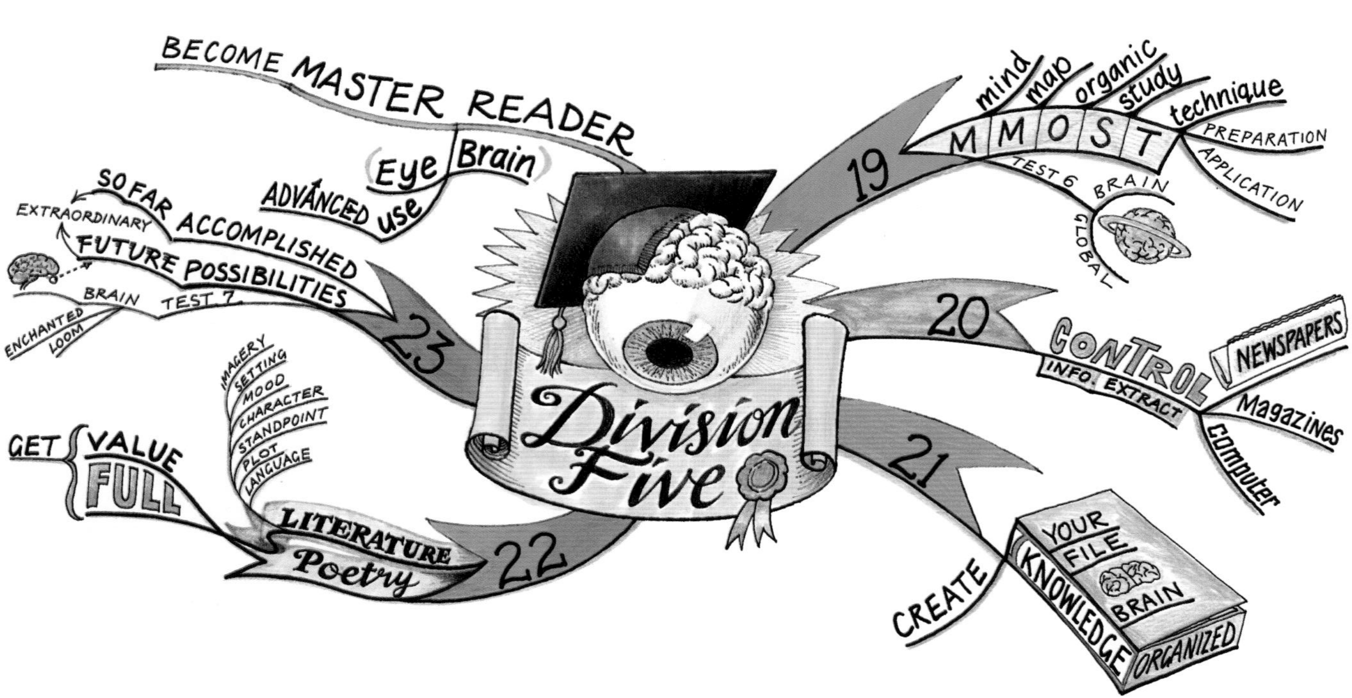

Plate VIII Mind Map of Division Five

CHAPTER NINE

Developing Your Advanced Skimming and Scanning Skills

The human visual system can photograph an entire page of print in one-twentieth of a second, and thus a standard-length book in between six and 25 seconds, and the entire Encyclopaedia Britannica *in less than an hour. Advanced skimming and scanning skills take you on the first step of this incredible journey.*

FOREWORD

Advanced **skimming** and **scanning** skills allow you to combine your already powerful meta-guiding techniques with a special emphasis on mental set – the way in which your brain can pre-select information for itself. This chapter clearly defines the differences between scanning and skimming, and also includes perception exercises which help to explain the concept of scanning as well as improving your scanning facility.

SCANNING

Scanning is when your eye glances over material in order to find a particular piece of information for which your brain is searching. Scanning is a simpler process than skimming, and is usually applied when you are looking up a word in the dictionary, a name or telephone number in the directory, or a particular piece of information in a textbook or report. The application of this technique is simple, as long as you make sure beforehand that you know the basic layout of the material you are scanning. This enables you to save the time that so many people spend hunting around in the wrong sections for the information they desire.

President Theodore Roosevelt was a renowned speed reader, known for his ability to get through far more reading material than his contemporaries. Dickens was one of Roosevelt's favourite authors, yet the president still applied scanning techniques when reading his novels. As Roosevelt said in one of his letters to his son Kermit: 'It always interests me about Dickens to think how almost all of it was mixed up with every kind of cheap, second-rate matter ... the wise thing to do is to simply skip the bosh and twaddle and vulgarity and untruth, and get the benefit out of the rest'!

Scanning is a natural skill. You do it every day of your life when you travel from point 'a' to point 'b', scanning the environment for directions, food, people, objects of danger and objects of fascination. In reading, scanning is a skill that grows rapidly with practice. The perception exercises at the end of this chapter will help in that regard, as will the information contained in Chapter 19, on the Mind Map Organic Study Technique (page 156).

SKIMMING

Skimming is more complex than scanning and is similar to the previewing techniques that will be discussed in later chapters. It can be defined as that process in which your eye covers certain pre-selected sections of the material in order to gain a *general overview* of that material.

The basic aim of skimming is to provide a fundamental architecture on which the 'bricks and mortar' can be placed. An excellent metaphor for skimming was developed by Dr Nila Banton Smith, of the Reading Institute of New York University. Under the title 'Swallows Skim – So Can You!' she continues:

> The swallow skims swiftly through the air, catching and devouring insects while simultaneously flapping his wings to propel his body. He even drinks as he skims along over brooks, ponds and rivers, gathering drops of water in his beak with no cessation in flight. This versatile creature doesn't pause or labour over any one insect or any one pool.
>
> The swallow's mode of skimming for food and water may be likened to the method used by skilled readers who skim over pages of print, gathering what they want as they 'fly' along. With instruction on practice a reader can become extremely adept in 'catching' what he desires from reading while 'on the wing'. This is the type of reading in which some people reach 1000 words per minute and are able to repeat the gist of what they have read.'

SUMMARY

1 Scanning is a process in which you look for *particular information*.
2 Skimming is a process in which you look for a *general overview*.
3 Both of these skills are used by the vast majority of speed readers.
4 Each these skills can be enhanced by the use of an advanced meta-guiding technique.

HIGH EYE-CUE ACTION POINTS

1 Spend ten minutes scanning a dictionary for words that you know and enjoy but cannot define precisely.
2 Practise scanning and skimming skills on everything you read from now on.

PERCEPTION EXERCISE 3

3 Complete the scanning exercises that follow below and on pages 100 to 102. Each page contains rows of numbers. The first number in each row is repeated somewhere across that row, and it is your task to spot it as quickly as possible. Start timing yourself. And, with the pencil in one hand, quickly check off the number in the row which corresponds to the number in the left-hand column. When you have done all the rows on that page, record your time at the bottom.

4 The exercises get more difficult as they progress, because the numbers get bigger and also more similar. By training in this way, you will be expanding the visual range of your 'mind's eye' which will help you develop both your skimming and scanning abilities.

5 You may do these exercises in small 'bites' or all at once if you wish. It is important when you do them that you be as mentally alert as possible, so make sure your eyes are 'fresh' and that you are highly motivated.

28	93	74	28	57	29	39	77
46	77	88	46	33	86	41	84
37	87	84	60	38	64	28	42
52	85	33	68	86	94	52	44
59	66	33	75	39	59	92	58
63	55	28	70	63	34	22	96
77	64	77	54	28	32	63	55
96	68	44	27	96	62	51	54
67	79	67	44	27	29	88	65
11	96	02	55	11	66	33	72
95	88	95	44	42	66	44	27
34	88	66	35	29	39	47	34
42	24	42	77	55	39	92	44
28	55	84	28	66	89	38	65
18	12	20	77	49	19	46	18
85	55	32	77	36	85	33	59
37	77	24	55	69	21	37	15
25	54	25	57	79	95	24	13
13	68	55	22	90	44	48	13
57	88	57	44	25	77	52	44
78	87	35	26	62	78	44	28
20	88	66	20	24	48	58	33
29	29	52	68	35	29	49	43

Time ....

675	568	675	875	639	891	569
625	874	271	018	625	735	906
672	672	875	236	438	282	239
911	743	343	554	277	911	902
764	543	674	764	246	665	322
879	772	544	754	272	879	647
753	258	266	372	753	348	236
844	766	343	568	844	236	543
877	565	235	877	655	235	568
822	544	822	654	266	388	419
103	202	547	103	654	813	113
457	790	235	252	457	746	322
238	198	674	368	238	636	638
848	765	638	848	636	426	853
847	784	737	636	782	844	847
336	772	327	874	336	764	873
379	673	838	379	737	892	811
282	537	282	987	254	654	272
444	765	238	444	266	782	754
658	690	343	562	676	658	824

Time ....

573	257	763	573	528	654	863
783	279	873	783	434	575	277
331	304	431	331	031	765	333
320	194	392	194	320	492	340
446	546	555	446	676	466	235
355	544	335	355	346	555	436
214	232	124	214	332	113	239
436	544	335	555	435	436	535
222	113	222	322	122	213	125
737	674	377	377	674	764	737
242	242	413	215	413	241	113
568	766	568	676	658	578	652
022	211	022	103	111	202	122
228	728	773	273	723	278	228
647	665	647	662	465	447	467
190	190	919	892	982	199	820
772	118	772	718	712	172	178
927	630	963	627	967	370	927
203	023	021	203	221	211	202
357	366	564	357	766	537	636

Time ....

120	992	192	117	911	200	120
554	336	354	554	332	552	355
013	121	103	022	013	105	212
483	485	483	249	429	825	843
217	613	622	262	217	127	617
528	726	276	528	753	258	573
2435	4427	6579	6755	2346	2435	2344
7877	7876	7868	7877	4568	3426	1988
3457	3457	7820	5433	7690	4564	2346
5683	3247	5622	5683	7622	8733	1957
1895	1949	1895	4527	7633	7683	1673
2215	2242	5623	6783	2212	2215	4125
5463	5463	8727	5673	7890	6533	0014
6782	1986	6722	6782	7629	9653	1935
5673	6582	8727	6739	6258	5268	5673
1873	1837	1873	8727	7628	1827	7828
2002	1003	0012	2002	1774	1021	1030
2680	8767	8687	6547	6438	2680	7444
7555	8665	5379	8677	7555	7677	5435
0865	0865	8766	7555	8776	5442	1645

Time ....

7524	6887	3568	4679	3479	5428	7524
8643	3569	8765	4589	8643	7544	3469
8532	6689	4489	8532	0166	1088	4672
8641	8651	6752	5572	7645	1754	8641
7302	1852	7411	7633	7302	0176	3467
3469	8533	4682	8752	3469	7632	8643
2458	7642	8644	4677	2458	8764	2476
7532	8642	3569	7644	1036	7532	8634
1876	1734	0568	8754	1876	8642	7433
8744	7533	7634	5689	8744	8754	3468
8756	8756	8876	5690	9756	4582	9752
8737	8762	8737	7755	7448	3569	7352
3469	7644	8876	3469	8754	1766	8442
1752	1751	1752	1742	8727	8764	8742
1978	1192	1978	7920	9772	8762	7792
8755	6755	8755	8548	8458	8745	8756
7654	7654	3368	3568	3568	5764	5369
1975	1975	1965	9148	7492	1948	1750
7865	7879	1756	7847	7865	4688	8747
8644	8649	8764	3487	8348	8644	3478

Time ....

8455	8456	8677	8455	4588	4585	8766
1176	1185	1766	1752	1158	1176	7642
8644	8638	8644	8642	4387	4369	8766
6433	2347	6434	6543	6433	3426	5433
8754	5785	8754	8763	4754	8736	3569
5242	8362	5413	7652	5242	8655	5243
7646	7655	7646	4766	5477	4578	5648
8412	8115	8412	1842	8712	4562	4812
8747	8765	4678	6489	7655	6875	8747
2575	2676	2676	2746	7453	4528	4453
7171	7702	7111	7172	7102	7171	0702
8742	7842	1875	8742	7815	1479	1785
4785	4789	4785	8748	8755	4785	4789
7633	7633	7624	2377	6738	2374	3729
3452	3435	3452	3542	1436	1544	5135
7634	7664	7337	7764	6734	7634	7637
8736	7854	6538	8736	8754	3579	9358

Time ....

ONWORD

The skimming and scanning skills you have just learnt are ideal for getting your brain into what Olympic athletes describe as a 'zone'. Prepare to multiply your already achieved excellencies in the next chapter, using the new Metronome Training Method.

CHAPTER TEN

Your Relativistic Brain –
Multiplying Your Speed by the New
Metronome Training Method

Your brain is a relativistic organ.

YOUR RELATIVISTIC BRAIN

If you were driving along a motorway at 100 miles per hour, and your partner suddenly covered your speedometer and asked you to decelerate to 20 miles per hour, at what speed do you think you would 'level off', saying 'That's 20 miles per hour'?

Most people estimate between 40 and 60 miles per hour and are correct.

The reason for this apparent absurdity is that the brain gets used to a *new norm*, and begins to compare all experiences with that norm. This extraordinary ability of your brain to adapt to any new norm is now being used in many areas, including Olympic training. In one instance runners were attached to a treadmill with a supporting belt. The treadmill was then gradually accelerated past their fastest speed to date, while they were encouraged to keep moving their legs at the appropriate speed. The supporting belt gave them a sense of security. After a series of such training sessions, many of them were able to break their previous records, because their brain/body system had become used to this new, speedier norm.

THE METRONOME TRAINING METHOD

The relativistic nature of your brain can also be applied to improving your reading speed by means of a metronome, which can be used in a number of ways. You can begin allowing each beat to indicate a single stroke along the line for your visual guide. In this way, a regular, steady, smooth reading rhythm can be established and maintained, and the usual deceleration in reading speed over time can be avoided. Once you have established a 'possible' reading speed, the metronome beat can be raised one beat per minute, and an improvement in your reading speed can be achieved.

A second major use of the metronome is for relativistic speed reading training. In this method of training, you set the metronome at an abnormally high speed, thereby obliging your eye/brain system to

103

become accustomed to a very high new norm. This form of training allows you to 'pull yourself up by the boot straps' by establishing very high new norms. You can then dip below them into comfortably 'slow' reading speeds which are still twice your previous average!

The High Eye-Cue section below contains a series of exercises designed to set you off on the high speed, high comprehension path!

SUMMARY
1 Your brain is a relativistic organ and can become used to accelerated norms.
2 The metronome reading and training method allows you to maintain and increase your reading speed.

HIGH EYE-CUE ACTION POINTS
In the following exercises, use whichever meta-guiding technique feels most appropriate.

1 Read normally for five minutes from a book which you will be able to continue using. Record your words per minute on your Progress Graph on page 187.

2 Use any book (light material) of your choice, preferably one in which you are interested.

Aim for as much comprehension as possible, but remember that this exercise is primarily concerned with speed. In this exercise, you should continue reading from the last point you reached.

(a) Practise-read for one minute at 100 wpm faster than your highest normal speed.
(b) Practise-read 100 wpm faster than (a).
(c) Practise-read 100 wpm faster than (b).
(d) Practise-read 100 wpm faster than (c).
(e) Practise-read 100 wpm faster than (d) in High Speed Practice 1.
(f) Practise-read with comprehension for one minute from the point reached at the end of (e). Calculate and record your wpm on your Progress graph.

3 High Speed Practice 1
(a) Use any easy book. Start from the beginning of a chapter.
(b) Practise-read with visual aid, three lines at a time at a *minimum* of 2000 wpm for five minutes. Mark the point where you stop.
(c) Re-read to mark in four minutes.
(d) Re-read to mark in three minutes.
(e) Re-read to mark in two minutes.
(f) Read on from mark, for same comprehension as at (b), for five minutes.

(g) Read for normal comprehension for one minute. Record your wpm on your Progress Graph.

4 High Speed Practice 2
(a) Using any easy book, start at the beginning of a chapter.
(b) Scan for one minute, using a visual aid and taking four seconds per page.
(c) Practise-read from the beginning at a minimum of 2000 wpm for five minutes.
(d) Repeat this exercise when possible.
(e) As 3 (g).

5 Exercise your eyes by moving them on horizontal and vertical planes diagonally upper left to lower right, and then upper right to lower left. Speed up gradually, day by day. The purpose of this exercise is to train your eyes to function more accurately and independently.

6 Practise turning 100 pages at approximately two seconds per page, moving your eyes very rapidly down the page. (Do this in two two-minute sessions.)

7 (a) Practise as fast as you can for one minute, not worrying about comprehension.
(b) Read with motivated comprehension – one minute.
(c) Calculate and record your wpm on your Progress Graph.

Repeat as time allows.

After you have completed a number of these Metronome Training exercises, go straight to Self Test 5 Before starting the reading proper, it might be an excellent idea to do a two-second-per-page 'Metronome Sprint' over the whole Self Test, as a skim and scan. When you start your actual reading, make sure your brain is especially well set for gathering more information about what you perceived in your 'Metronome Sprint'.

SELF TEST 5   Baby Brain
by Dr Sue Whiting
The early development of the baby brain is a period of intense neural activity when brain cell interconnections are being forged at a furious pace. It is never too early for the brain to start learning.

Brain Spurts
The brain takes longer than any other organ to reach its full development, and its growth pattern is markedly different. In most other organs, basic development is completed in the womb. Further growth in size is through the cellular division as the body grows. The

brain, on the other hand, has its full complement of cells before birth – that is why the heads of babies seem out of proportion to the rest of their bodies.

Research carried out during the last ten years builds on previous evidence that the brain begins elaborating on the connections between cells whilst still in the womb, using spontaneously generated signals. At about eight weeks after conception, the first of the 'brain spurts' begins (the term 'brain spurt' relates to increased development of the brain). Over the next five weeks the majority of nerve cells are formed. The second 'brain spurt' begins approximately ten weeks before birth and continues for about two years after birth. The second spurt is a period of intense activity for the brain cells: interconnections are refined, tuned and expanded. This increase in connectivity results in a rapid growth of the brain. At birth it weighs 25 per cent of its adult weight, at six months it is 50 per cent, at two and a half years 75 per cent and at five years 90 per cent.

Introduction to the World
Studies have shown that a child responds positively and specifically to the tones of the human voice at birth. A high-speed film of a newborn baby, when slowed down and examined frame by frame, shows that tiny gestures on the part of the child are synchronized with specific tones and syllables from the parent(s). Sounds other than the human voice produce no such response. This implies that some linguistic skills are learnt while in the womb. Having heard the mother's heart while in the womb, this sound is recognized by the baby and has a soothing effect.

Tom Bower's research on infant perception at the University of Edinburgh shows that a child experiences a three-dimensional world from birth. Using polarizing goggles so that the left and right eye see different images, he created the visual illusion that there was a solid object in front of the baby. Bower found that even newborn babies stretched out their hands to touch the apparent object, but as soon as their hand closed upon empty air instead of a solid object the baby started crying. This shows that at birth a child expects visual objects to be tangible, and indicates a simple unity of the visual and tactile senses.

Sight and Sound
Other experiments at Edinburgh have shown that sight and sound are also integrated, the newborn turning its head in the direction of a sound, especially the mother's voice. They have shown that a baby is also born with the ability to recognize smells as pleasant or unpleasant, turning its head toward or away as appropriate.

The newborn child can also recognize a human face. Robert Frantz, a researcher at Western Reserve University in Cleveland, presented day-old children with the choice of looking at a picture of a face, a bull's eye, newsprint, or coloured circles. He found a preference for the human face, most of the babies looking at it far more than the other objects. Mark Johnson, of Carnegie Mellion, carried out similar tests on infants as young as ten minutes; and observed a marked preference for pictures of faces to pictures of blank ovals or faces with scrambled features. This implies, according to Johnson, that humans are born with a 'template' of a face which helps us to discern the source of food, warmth and protection.

Babies who are spoken to as human beings, rather than just cooed at, have a much greater opportunity to pick up language. A rich early environment, where one or both parents consciously aim to develop their child's sensory experience, can speed up and enhance development. As early as 1952, Aaron Stern decided his daughter, Edith, could benefit from a consciously stimulating environment. From birth, he talked to her as much as possible (not baby talk), played classical music, and showed her flash cards with numbers and animals on them. This technique has been adapted and used by countless other parents, with very positive results.

Ramps, Ladders and Wheels

To assess the effect of a rich environment on brain growth, Mark Rosenweig, at the University of California at Berkeley, allowed a group of baby rats to grow up in a cage full of ramps, ladders, wheels, tunnels and other stimuli. A second group was left in barren cages. After 105 days the brains were examined, showing the brains of the rats raised in the rich environment to have more connections than the control group. There were also 15 per cent more cells, and the neurone bodies were 15 per cent larger, and, perhaps most importantly, there were more interconnections with other neurones.

The belief in biologically programmed core knowledge lies at the heart of most baby development research, not only with mathematics and physics, but with other cognitive skills. Just when such core knowledge is programmed is as yet uncertain. Since 1988, when a special multi-electrode device was invented at the California Institute of Technology, it has been more possible to detect and measure cells in the brains of mammal foetuses firing impulses to each other, making, tuning and adapting connections while in the womb. Work carried out on such neural activity suggests that it is during the 'brain spurts' that the interconnections are developed, rather than each neural connection being stored in our genes. Given the millions of connections which need to be formed in the brain, the former theory would need much less genetic information to be stored. It would imply that genetic blueprints are worked on as the baby is in the womb and during infancy.

107

Nature Versus Nurture

The above is a relatively new hypothesis. Much work needs to be carried out to develop and demonstrate it. It would add a vital new insight into the nature and nurture debate.

In a field of research which involves a multitude of theories, studies and conclusions, revelations of the potential of babies given the right stimuli will continue to encourage parents. The vital influence of nurture gives all parents the chance to help their offspring as much as they can, in whatever way they see fit and feasible.

Whether due to genetic programming, or whether due to the inter-connections made between neurones whilst still in the womb and during the critical first few months, our awareness of babies' mental abilities and capabilities is growing. Whatever ways parents find to encourage and enhance their children's mental development, two key points must be considered.

Firstly, continuity must be observed. A child whose abilities are more developed than those of his or her schoolmates may deliberately hold back, in order not to appear different or to avoid jealous derision.

Secondly, care must be taken to truly respect the developing child's wishes and interests. Having invested a lot of time, emotion and hopes, parents must be aware of not putting too much control on how the fruits of their labour are used. The main issue is the happiness and fulfilment of the child, and the joy of parenting lies in taking an active part.

∗ ∗

Stop Your Timer Now
Length of time: .... mins

Next, calculate your reading speed in words per minute (wpm) by simply dividing the number of words in the passage (in this case 1256) by the time (in minutes) you took.

Speed Reading Formula:
words per minute (wpm) = $\dfrac{\text{number of words}}{\text{time}}$

When you have completed your calculation, enter the number in the wpm slot at the end of this paragraph, and enter it on your Progress Chart and your Progress Graph on page 187.

Words per minute: ....

SELF TEST 5: COMPREHENSION

1 The human brain:
(a) has a full complement of cells at conception
(b) has a full complement of cells before birth
(c) has a full complement of cells one month after birth
(d) has a full complement of cells two years after birth

2 The first of the 'brain spurts' begins:
(a) at conception
(b) eight weeks after conception
(c) four months after conception
(d) one month before birth

3 The second 'brain spurt' begins approximately:
(a) eight weeks after conception
(b) ten weeks after conception
(c) ten weeks before birth
(d) four weeks before birth

4 At birth the human brain weighs:
(a) 10 per cent
(b) 15 per cent
(c) 25 per cent
(d) 40 per cent
of its adult weight

5 At six months the brain weighs:
(a) 25 per cent
(b) 40 per cent
(c) 50 per cent
(d) 75 per cent
of its adult weight

6 At two and a half years the brain weighs:
(a) 50 per cent
(b) 75 per cent
(c) 80 per cent
(d) 90 per cent
of its adult weight

7 At five years the human brain weighs:
(a) 85 per cent
(b) 90 per cent
(c) 95 per cent
(d) 100 per cent
of its adult weight

8 The human baby can respond positively and specifically to tones of the human voice on the day of its birth.   True/False

9 Tom Bower's research on infant perception at the University of Edinburgh shows that at birth a child:
(a) sees only blurred images
(b) immediately focuses on its mother
(c) can hear sounds well
(d) experiences a three-dimensional world immediately

10 Other experiments at Edinburh have shown that sight and sound are also integrated, a newborn turning its head in the direction of the sound, especially ....

11 Robert Frantz and Mark Johnson discovered that a newborn child showed a marked preference for pictures of:
(a) its mother
(b) coloured circles
(c) faces
(d) animals

12 Children who are 'cooed' at have a much greater opportunity to pick up language.   True/False

13 Mark Rosenweig's experiments with rats showed that those in an enriched environment:
(a) had smaller brains
(b) grew physically bigger
(c) had no changes in their brains
(d) had more connections between brain cells

14 Neural interconnections are developed in the baby's brain:
(a) during 'brain spurts'
(b) before birth
(c) from storage compartments in our genes
(d) during the first two years of life

15 The main issue in parenting is:
(a) developing a genius
(b) providing a good academic education
(c) the happiness and fulfilment of the child
(d) not interfering with the child's natural development

Check your answers against those on page 185.
Then divide your score by 15 and multiply by 100
to calculate your percentage comprehension.

Comprehension score: .... out of 15
.... per cent

Now enter your score on your Progress Chart and your Progress Graph on page 187.

ONWORD
You have completed **Division 2 – Your Amazing Eyes**. Armed with state-of-the-art information about the astonishing range of abilities and sophistication of your eyes, and with techniques for getting the maximum benefit from your eye/brain system, you are now ready to tackle the main 'problem areas' in reading: lack of concentration; lack of comprehension; and the various, usually misnamed 'learning difficulty' syndromes.

CHAPTER ELEVEN

The Common Reading Problems – Sub-Vocalization, Finger-Pointing, Regression and Back-Skipping

Once a problem is faced, analysed and understood, it becomes a positive energy centre for the creation of solutions.

FOREWORD

This chapter discusses some of the most frequently mentioned reading problems – **sub-vocalization**, **finger-pointing**, **regression**, and **back-skipping** – which are all major barriers to efficient reading. New approaches, based on the most recent research on the functioning and relationship of the eye and brain, are offered to correct much of what has been written on these subjects.

In addition this chapter deals with the two most common 'learning difficulty' areas: **dyslexia** and **ADDS** (Attention Disability Disorder Syndrome, also known as Attention Deficit Disorder Syndrome).

READING PROBLEMS

Sub-Vocalization

A common reading problem is sub-vocalization, the tendency to 'mouth' the words you are reading. It is caused by the way in which children are taught to read: usually by the phonetic or phonic method or the look-say method, as discussed in Chapter 2

Virtually every book and course on speed reading maintains that this habit is one of the greatest barriers to improvement and that it *must* be overcome.

However the truth of the matter is that we can benefit from sub-vocalization. It does, undoubtedly, hold the reader back in certain circumstances, especially when he is dependent upon it for understanding, but this is not necessary. In the real sense of the word sub-vocalization *cannot* and should not be completely eliminated. Once this is understood, the 'problem' may be approached in its proper perspective, leading to much more satisfactory reading habits. People who are instructed to 'eliminate sub-vocalization' often become discouraged and lose their enjoyment of reading altogether after spending weeks attempting to accomplish the impossible.

The proper approach to this problem is to accept that, while sub-vocalization *always* persists, it can be pushed further and further back into the 'semi-conscious'. In other words, while never being able to eliminate the habit completely, you can become less dependent upon it. This means that you need not worry when you occasionally realize that you are sub-vocalizing, because it is a universal habit. What you should try to do is to become less dependent on this habit for complete understanding.

A positive side to it is that you can actually use sub-vocalization as an aid to remembering what you have read. Assuming that practice has enabled you to become less dependent on sub-vocalization, you can consciously increase the 'volume' of your sub-vocalization when reading important words or concepts ('shouting' them internally), thus making those bits of information stand out from the rest.

In addition to this, it will help you to realize that sub-vocalization is not, by definition, a slow, plodding process. It is quite possible for your brain to sub-vocalize as many as 2000 words per minute. Indeed there are now actually a number of people who can *speak* at above 1000 words per minute. So only start worrying, if it is your choice to worry, when you reach these speeds!

Finger-Pointing

Finger-pointing has only traditionally been considered a problem because of our misconception that it slows the reader down. You now know, from Chapters 6, 7 and 8, that finger-pointing is an excellent method of maintaining concentration and focus. The only disadvantage is that the physical size of the finger and hand block the view. Thus the 'problem' suggests the solution, the use of a slim guide making the habit a perfect one for accelerated reading speeds.

Regression and Back-Skipping

Regression and back-skipping are similar but distinct. Regression is a conscious returning to words, phrases or paragraphs you feel you have missed or misunderstood. Many readers feel they must return to them in order to understand the material. Back-skipping is a kind of visual tic, an unconscious skipping back to words or phrases that have just been read. You are almost never aware that you are back-skipping.

As outlined in Chapter 4 on eye movements, back-skipping and regression add to the number of fixations per line, slowing down the reading process. Both these habits are usually unnecessary. Studies performed on the conscious re-reading of material indicate that readers who were *sure* they needed to return to certain words or sections in order to understand them showed little change in their comprehension scores when not allowed to do so. It is not so much a matter of comprehension as of having confidence in your brain's ability.

The approach to eliminating or reducing these two habits is twofold. Firstly, you must *force* yourself not to re-read sections you think you may have missed. Secondly, you must gradually push up your speed, trying to maintain an even rhythm in your eye movements. Both speed and rhythm will make back-skipping and regression more difficult, while actually improving your comprehension.

These problem areas – sub-vocalization, finger-pointing, back-skipping and regressing – may now no longer be seen as the major barriers so many people have made them out to be. They are simply habits that can be adjusted and, in many cases, used to great advantage.

LEARNING PROBLEMS

Dyslexia

Dyslexia is a term commonly applied to a person who has difficulty in decoding letters of the alphabet, and consequently reading words. They often get letters reversed, and will tend to have scrawly handwriting. In some schools and school districts, more than 20 per cent of children are labelled with this 'learning disability'.

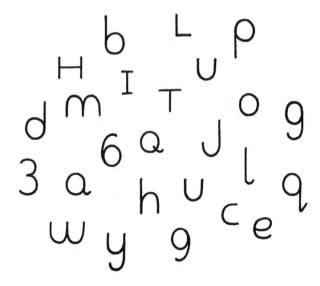

Fig. 12 Hard to learn shapes that can result in a misdiagnosis of dsylexia in the beginning reader. *See opposite.*

114

In my own experience more than 80 per cent of those I have met who have been labelled dyslexic were not. They had simply stumbled at one of the many early stages of their reading career, and had never been allowed to get up.

To realize how easy it is to fall at an early stage, imagine that you are a Martian. You land, completely innocent, on the planet Earth and someone rapidly explains to you that these particular space beings have a series of random shapes that they call letters, and which they put into words. Just to make things more difficult, many of the shapes are incredibly similar (see Fig.12, opposite).

(To understand how difficult the task is, try the following exercise. Rapidly point to each of the different shapes, moving from one to the next as fast as you can, naming them accurately as you go. Most people find that, sooner or later, they stumble and mis-identify one of them.)

You are now back as a Martian, having been told the names of these various squiggles, and you are asked to write the word 'god'. You search your memory banks, and vaguely remember that the three letters probably have a circle in them. Writing down three circles, '000', you then also vaguely remember that there seemed to be an upward stick and a downward stick somewhere in there, so on the first one you put an upward stick on the right-hand side of the circle and on the last one a downward stick also on the right-hand side. Confidently believing that you are nearly if not perfectly correct, you hand in your paper, only to be greeted with derision and the statement that you are probably dyslexic, or, to put it more brutally, suffering from some minor form of brain damage.

This would obviously put you into a particularly tense frame of mind, increasing the probability that you would make a mistake on your next attempt.

This scenario is precisely what has happened to the majority of people labelled dyslexic, and all because, in the beginning, they were not given the tools necessary for memory, namely association and image, which would have enabled them to recall the names of the letters easily. Their first mistake fitted into the definition of dyslexia, and they were falsely labelled, entering a downward spiral that made them get worse as their academic careers progressed.

Very often the person labelled dyslexic tries to read more slowly and carefully in order to gain better comprehension, thereby unwittingly making the problem even worse (see Chapter 4, page 40).

If you have ever been labelled dyslexic, the following three brief stories will give you hope.

A 16-year-old girl in the Scandinavian School of Brussels attended a Buzan Centre course on Mind Mapping and Learning, and on the first day did exceptionally well. On the morning of the second day she came up to the teacher and asked to be excused from the morning session, because it was on speed reading and she couldn't read very well at all 'because she was dyslexic' and because, as she put it, 'I can't really read properly'. The teacher encouraged her to give it a try, which she did. The result? From an initial reading speed of 100 words per minute and poor comprehension, she graduated at the end of the day with a speed of 600 words per minute and 70 per cent comprehension.

The second story concerns a script editor who described her school years as 'sheer hell'. Having failed to learn reading properly at school, she had been utterly devastated, because she loved reading and literature. Being of a persistent frame of mind, she stuck to her reading tasks, working extra hours at a pace at least four times as slow as her contemporaries.

Her dream had always been to be a script editor, a job which she finally managed to acquire. However, after six months, she was beginning to sink because she had to spend not only her full working day, but most of the night, working through her reading material in order to keep up with the pace demanded by the job.

Like the Scandinavian girl, she started with a reading speed of 100 words per minute and very poor comprehension. Throughout the course she had kept her 'secret' private. At the end of the final reading test, she had increased her speed to 700 words per minute with good comprehension. She stood up the instant she had calculated her final speed, and told her story. Everyone had expected her to be only thrilled, but she was trembling from head to foot.

She explained that, for her entire life, she had been embarrassed by her incompetence and inability, and that suddenly all that was disappearing, and it was cause for celebration.

At the same time, however, she was experiencing an almost uncontrollable fury about her wasted years, her lifetime of humiliation, and her sudden realization that the dyslexic label had abused her and kept her in a mental prison. And all of it unnecessary.

The happy ending to the story is that she returned to her job, and was able to complete her daily tasks in *less* than normal working hours.

The third and final story concerns Kim, an executive with the University of Texas Medical Board. Attending a Mind Mapping and Speed Reading course run by Vanda North, Kim explained at the beginning that she suffered from severe dyslexia and would probably not be able to complete many of the course modules. Her initial reading speed was 120 words per minute with very low comprehension.

Yet Kim persevered and was successful, reaching a very credible 750 words per minute with excellent comprehension at the end of the two days. The course had also involved a section on presentation skills, and each of the members was required, in the final celebration ceremony, to give a brief presentation.

Kim left the room in order to prepare.

After a few minutes she returned, covered in labels that read 'stupid', 'slow', 'dumb', 'worthless', 'backward', 'ESN', 'dyslexic', 'failure' and 'idiot'. One by one, she ripped them off, using slow-motion mime, grimacing as she did so and exulting as each one was removed. Her whole presentation was performed in total silence.

There was not a dry eye in the room.

As I have said, most people labelled dyslexic are not, and even if they actually are, the fundamental solution to their reading problems is the same: use a guide, gradually accelerate the speed, and escape the semantic prison of sentences by using Mind Maps as a note-taking and thinking device. At the time of writing, neither I nor any of my teachers have found anyone, either falsely or correctly labelled as dyslexic, who was not able to improve their reading speed and comprehension by significant amounts.

ADDS and Hyperactivity

A great deal of controversy surrounds Attention Disability Disorder Syndrome and hyperactivity.

One terrifying statistic confirms that, in America alone, over three million children have been diagnosed as having the disorder so seriously that they are on the drug Ritalin.

The debate rages as to whether the syndrome exists as a medically definable illness, whether it is a dangerous generalized diagnosis made by ignorant doctors, whether teachers are sticking the ADDS and hyperactive labels on children as a cover-up for their own inability to maintain the child's interest, and whether Ritalin is a miracle drug or one that is normalizing, numbing and drugging fundamentally active and creative children into a conformist stupor.

To help you draw your own conclusions, the following information may prove useful.

ADHD, Attention Deficit Hyperactivity Disorder, is defined, by the American Psychiatric Association and others, as a classifiable illness if an individual meets eight or more of the following criteria:

1 Cannot remain seated if required to do so.
2 Is easily distracted by external stimuli.
3 Experiences difficulty focusing on a single task or play activity.
4 Frequently begins another activity without completing the first (it is interesting to note that Leonardo da Vinci, normally regarded as the greatest genius of all time, and ranked number one in *Buzan's Book of Genius*, was consistently accused of this!).
5 Fidgets or squirms (or feels restless mentally).

117

6 Can't (or doesn't want to) wait for his or her turn during group activities.
7 Will often interrupt with an answer before a question is completed.
8 Has problems with chores or following through on a job.
9 Likes to make noises while playing.
10 Interrupts others inappropriately.
11 Talks impulsively or excessively.
12 Doesn't seem to listen when spoken to by a teacher.
13 Impulsively jumps into physically dangerous activities.
14 Regularly loses things (pencils, tools, papers) necessary to complete school work projects.

These forms of behaviour must have commenced before the age of seven, and must occur more frequently than in the average person of the same age.

This means that *at least half the population* will, by definition, exhibit these forms of behaviour more frequently than the average. Are they all therefore suffering from an illness?!

Two classic cases are worth bearing in mind.

As a young girl in kindergarten, Mary-Lou Retton was so super-active that her parents were advised by the school teachers to put her on a course of drugs that would dramatically reduce her physical activity. Fortunately her parents were of a different opinion, and requested that the school find ways of using her extraordinary energy more appropriately.

Thirteen years later, Mary-Lou Retton, internationally renowned for her boundless energy and enthusiasm, easily won the gold medal in women's gymnastics at the Los Angeles Olympics.

A few years before Mary-Lou Retton experienced her difficulties in her early school years, a little boy by the name of Daley was experiencing the same problems in England. Similarly, his parents were encouraged to put him on a course of tranquillizing drugs. Like Mary-Lou's parents, Daley's insisted that he be given exercises and activities that would absorb his ebullience. Little Daley proved virtually indefatigable, wearing out every physical education teacher available.

It all paid off wonderfully well when Daley Thompson became the World and Olympic Decathlon Champion and stayed at the peak of his sport, shattering all previous world records consistently, for ten years.

Thom Hartmann, in his excellent book *Attention Deficit Disorder: A Different Perception*, is firmly of the opinion that the labels are often wildly inappropriate. Hartmann claims that schools are set up for what he terms 'the farmers' – those who will sit at a desk, watch and listen attentively to the teacher, and always do what they are told. This is the ultimate torture for those he labels the 'hunters' who are physically active; always scanning their environment; creative; impulsive; and always looking, like Leonardo da Vinci, for the next exciting event.

Whether or not you think you suffer from dyslexia or hyperactivity, there are some general pointers that will allow you to concentrate and comprehend more easily. These will be dealt with in Chapter 12

SUMMARY
All reading problems and learning difficulties can be dealt with and the situation improved. In most cases the problems can be completely overcome.

HIGH EYE-CUE ACTION POINTS
1 Continue to use your guide to help you reduce regression and back-skipping.
2 Use sub-vocalization as a memory device.
3 If you have been labelled dyslexic, hyperactive or suffering from Attention Deficit Disability Syndrome, get rid of the labels!
4 If you are an adult, don't label any child 'disordered' in any way. Children react strongly to labels, especially to negative ones, often more than adults. Explaining that a child has a 'deficit or disorder' will usually be more destructive than helpful.
5 Repeat the metronome training exercises on pages 104 and 105.

ONWORD
As well as poor reading speed, lack of concentration and comprehension are regularly listed as the major reading problems that people have around the world. The next chapter gives you insights on how to improve your performance in these areas.

CHAPTER TWELVE

Improving Your Concentration and Increasing Your Comprehension

The power to maintain their concentration is claimed by many of the world's Great Brains to be the prime factor in their success. When you master this, your eye/brain system becomes laser-like in its ability to focus and absorb. Your capacity to do this is, according to researchers in the field, infinite.

FOREWORD

Having tackled some basic reading problems, we are now ready to discuss what causes poor **concentration** and **comprehension** and suggest ways in which they can be maximized. I shall also introduce the revolutionary concept that *no one* has a problem with concentration!

THE IMPORTANCE OF READING GOALS

An interesting example of one of the great historical geniuses applying his enormous concentration powers to the task of reading is that of President Thomas Jefferson, widely regarded as the greatest all-round intellect ever produced by the United States of America.

Professor Robert Zorn reports that Jefferson believed in mapping out his reading into a definite plan of action, defining specific goals for each topic that he covered, and never allowing himself to deviate from his reading schedule until he had completed the task. No distractions, no dissipation of time by 'scattered inattentiveness' were the keys to Jefferson's methodology and to his unparalleled powers of concentration. Jefferson further believed that a good reader should choose a course of reading with a definite purpose, whether that be to hunt out specific knowledge, to cultivate the mind, or for recreation.

Jefferson offered this advice to the reader: you should know 'where you are, and what you are doing, and what time it is, and whether you are falling short of your schedule or not, and, if so, how far short.'

Jefferson also described his reading speed as 'always calm, even stately, like the tick of a tall mahogany clock'. Jefferson had intuitively recognized and foreseen the development of rhythmical reading and the metronome method!

This chapter will enable you to approach Jefferson's extraordinary concentration and comprehension levels.

WHAT CAUSES POOR CONCENTRATION?

The many reasons for lack of concentration when reading include vocabulary difficulties, conceptual difficulty of the material, inappropriate reading speed, incorrect mental set, poor organization, lack of interest, and lack of motivation.

Vocabulary Difficulties

Once you have increased your vocabulary with the information and exercises in Chapters 16, 17 and 18, you will already be on the way to solving this one. In addition, if the material you are reading continually confronts you with words which you do not understand or understand only vaguely, your concentration will gradually become worse because the ideas you are trying to absorb will be interrupted by gaps in understanding. A smooth inflow of information, unhampered by the lurking fear of misunderstanding, is a necessity for efficient reading. The vocabulary analysis and exercises in this book are designed to overcome this difficulty.

If you come to a word that you do not understand, just underline it and read on.

Usually the meaning becomes vaguely apparent from the context of the sentence. Then, at the end of the chapter or that day's reading, you can do a 'Dictionary Run' and look them all up at the same time.

Conceptual Difficulty of the Material

This is a slightly more difficult problem to overcome and usually arises in academic books. The best approach is to 'multiple read' the material using the information on the guide in Chapter 6. Skimming, scanning, paragraph structure and previewing are discussed thoroughly in Chapter 9, 14 and 15 and in *Use Your Head*.

Inappropriate Reading Speed

This is often a product of the school system. When children are given important or difficult material, they are usually told: 'Read this *slowly* and *carefully*.' This approach establishes a vicious circle, because the more slowly one reads the less one understands, which makes the material seem even more incomprehensible. Ultimately a point of complete frustration is reached and the material is often abandoned in despair.

If you have poor concentration and comprehension this may well be the problem, so vary your speeds on difficult material, trying to go faster rather than more slowly, and you may find a great improvement. By learning to speed and range read, you will have control and choice of the appropriate speed for the material, needs, time of day, energy level and internal and external environments.

Incorrect Mental Set

This simply means that your mind has not really been directed in the best way toward the material you are trying to read. You may, for instance, still be concentrating on an argument that took place in the office, or a social engagement for the coming evening.

What you must try to do is to 'shake out' the unnecessary threads that are running through your mind, and direct yourself to think actively about the subject you are reading. You may even go so far as to stop for a moment and consciously gather together your thoughts. One way to do this most efficiently is to do a rapid two-minute Mind Map (see Chapter 13) on the topic you are studying in order to re-collect your thoughts and to provide you with an even stronger ongoing mental set. We shall be examining the question of mental set in greater detail in Chapter 19.

Poor Organization

This problem is far more common than many people realize. Actually getting down to reading a book is a battle of the will, and almost demands a run-up to the desk in order to gain enough impetus actually to sit down at it. Having arrived and started to read many people suddenly realize that they don't have a pencil, notepaper, their glasses and any number of other things, and consequently disrupt their concentration to get these materials.s

The solution is easy: before you sit down to read, make sure that all the materials you will need are readily available (see Chapter 5).

Lack of Interest

This is a problem most often experienced by students or people taking special courses and we devote special attention to it in our reading courses. The first step in solving it is to review the points discussed in this chapter, for lack of interest is often related to other difficulties. For instance, interest will be difficult to maintain if a deficient vocabulary is continually interrupting understanding, if the material is confusing, if other thoughts keep popping up, and if the necessary materials are not available.

Assuming that these problems are overcome and that your interest is still not as high as it should be, you need to analyse your personal approach to the material.

Firstly, make sure that the technique being used is appropriate (see the Mind Map Organic Study Technique described in Chapter 19).

If this fails, you can try the 'severe critic' approach. Rather than reading the material as you normally would, get annoyed at it for having presented you with problems and try to analyse it thoroughly, concentrating especially on the negative aspects. You will find yourself actually becoming interested in the material, much in the way that you become interested in listening to the arguments of someone whom you don't particularly like and wish to oppose vigorously!

Lack of Motivation

This is a different problem, often stemming from having no clearly defined purpose to your reading. Once you have analysed your reasons for reading the book or article, your motivation may automatically increase. Alternatively, you may conclude that you need not read it at all. If your reasons are valid, there may indeed be no point in reading the book, but make sure they are really valid!

YOUR CONCENTRATION STALLION

In my 25 years lecturing around the world on speed reading skills, I have found that literally 999 per cent of people admit to having problems with concentration.

This problem regularly manifests itself in periods of daydreaming, which occur at least once every 30 to 40 minutes. Once again, our inappropriate training has made us see something which is actually good, in a bad light. When your brain daydreams after 30 or 40 minutes, it is doing exactly what it should – taking a break at exactly the right time.

So, in most cases, it is not a question of losing concentration, but a more positive matter of taking a break when you should.

Let us, though, examine what actually happens when you 'lose concentration' while reading a book: what *actually* happens is that you **concentrate** on a few pages of the book, after which you **concentrate** on someone walking by, after which you **concentrate** on a few more lines or pages of the book, after which you **concentrate** on a bird landing on a tree outside your window, after which you **concentrate** on the book again, after which you **concentrate** on your fingernail, after which you **concentrate** on the book again, after which you **concentrate** on a daydream, after which you **concentrate** on the book once more.

Throughout the entire period you have been **CONCENTRATING!**

The problem is not with your **concentration,** for you are **concentrating** 100 per cent of the time. The problem is with the *direction* and *focus* of that perfect concentration.

Concentration can thus be seen as a wild stallion, with you as the rider. In most instances, the stallion has its way, going off at full gallop in whatever direction it pleases. As a masterful rider/reader, it is up to you to rein in the stallion of your concentration, steering it in the direction appropriate to the reading task at hand.

SUMMARY
1 Problems with concentration are caused not by inherent inabilities, but by the difficulties caused by an incomplete education in reading.
2 Concentration is like a stallion. You are always riding it. It is up to you to become a good rider!

HIGH EYE-CUE ACTION POINTS
1 Take breaks every 30 to 60 minutes in order to improve concentration and give your eyes and brain a needed rest.
2 Improve your vocabulary (see Chapters 16, 17 and 18). When you do you will improve your reading speed and comprehension.
3 Check that your reading speeds are appropriate to the material you are reading.
4 Make sure you establish appropriate goals before you start to read.
5 Make sure that your environment is appropriately organized for your reading task.
6 By whatever method, raise your levels of interest and motivation!
7 Continue to practise and use a guide for increased concentration and comprehension.

ONWORD
Now that your visual skills are rapidly improving, and your concentration stallion is under your control, you are ready to move on to **Division 4 – Developing Advanced Speed Reading Skills.**

In this division you will learn a reading and thinking technique known as 'the Swiss army knife of the brain', Mind Mapping, as well as how to use knowledge of paragraph structure to increase your speed and comprehension. This will be supplemented by the technique of previewing. You will also be given the major keys to unlock your vocabulary power – one of the prime factors in overall reading success.

CHAPTER THIRTEEN

Mind Mapping®: A New Dimension in Thinking and Note-Taking

For centuries the human race has noted and recorded for the following purposes: memory; communication; problem-solving and analysis; creative thinking; and summarization. The techniques that have been used to do this include sentences, lists, lines, words, analysis, logic, linearity, numbers and monotonic (one colour) usage.

Good though some of these systems may seem, they all use what you now know to be the dominantly 'left cortical' thought modalities. When you begin to use these necessary elements in conjunction with rhythm, dimension, colour, space and imagination, all your mental skills will increase significantly and your mind will begin to reflect its true majesty.

FOREWORD
How often have you seen 'the diligent student' hanging on every word that his teacher or professor utters, and faithfully recording each gem in his notebook?! It is a fairly common sight, and one that brings a number of negative consequnces. This chapter explains the **disadvantages of normal note-taking** and introduces you to **the Mind Map**, a revolutionary new note-taking technique.

THE DISADVANTAGES OF NORMAL NOTE-TAKING
First, the person who is intent on getting everything down is like the reader who does not preview – he inevitably fails to see the forest (the general flow of argument) for the trees.

Second, a continuing preoccupation with getting things down prevents objective and ongoing critical analysis and appreciation of the subject matter. All too often, note-taking bypasses the mind altogether, in much the same way as a secretary can type an entire novel and not have the faintest idea of what it was about.

And third, the volume of notes taken in this manner tends to become so enormous (especially when combined with added notes from books), that when it comes to 'revising', the student finds he almost has to do the whole task again.

Proper note-taking is not a slavish following of what has been said or written, but *a selective process* which should minimize the volume of words taken down, and maximize the amount remembered from those words.

To achieve this, we make use of key words. A key word is a word that encapsulates a multitude of meanings in as small a unit as possible. When that word is triggered, the meanings spray free (see Fig.13, below).

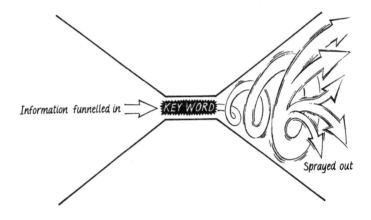

Fig. 13 How key words work in assisting note-taking and memory.

Selecting key words is easy. The first stage is to eliminate all the unnecessary surrounding language, so that if you came across the following statement in a science text: 'The speed of light has now been determined to be 186,000 miles per second' you would not write the whole sentence down but would summarize it as follows: 'light's speed = 186,000 mps'.

It is important to remember when making your notes with key words that the key-recall-words *must* trigger the right kind of remembering. In this respect words like 'beautiful' and 'horrifying', while being picturesque, are too general. They have many other meanings which might have nothing to do with the particular point you wish to remember.

Further, a key word should be one that you find personally satisfying and not just one which you think somebody else might think is good. In many cases key words need not be taken directly from the content of the lecture or the material being read. A word that you choose yourself, and which effectively summarizes somebody else's words, is preferable.

If you practise key word note-taking effectively you will be amazed at how much more information you can get into a given space.

THE MIND MAP® – A NEW DIMENSION IN NOTE-TAKING

A Mind Map draws on all your mental skills: the associative and imaginative skills from your memory; the words, numbers, lists, sequences, logic and analyis from your left cortex; the colour, imagery, dimension, rhythm, daydreaming, gestalt (whole picture) and spatial awareness abilities of the right side of your cortex; the power of your eyes to perceive and assimilate; the power of your hands, with increasing skill, to duplicate what your eyes have seen; and the power of your whole brain to organize, store and recall that which it has learnt.

In Mind Map notes, instead of taking down what you wish to remember in the normal sentence or list fashion, you place an image in the centre of the page (to help your concentration and memory) and then branch out in an organized way around that image, using key words and key images. As you continue to build up the Mind Map, your brain creates an integrated map of all the intellectual territory you are exploring.

The rules for a Mind Map are as follows:

1 A coloured image in the centre.

2 Main ideas branch off the centre.

3 Main ideas should be in larger letters than secondary ideas.

4 Always have one word per line. Each word has an enormous number of associations, and this rule allows each one more freedom to link to other associations in your brain.

5 Words should always be printed (either in upper or lower, or a combination of upper and lower case).

6 Words should always be printed on the lines (this gives your brain a clearer image to remember).

7 Lines should be connected (this helps your memory to associate). The connected lines should be the same length as the word or image for efficiency of both association and space.

8 Use as many images as possible (this helps develop a whole-brained approach, as well as making it much easier for your memory; a picture is, in this context, worth a thousand words).

9 Use dimension wherever possible (things that stand out are more easily remembered).

10 Use numbers or codes or put things in order, or show connections.

11 For coding and connecting, use arrows, symbols, numbers, letters, images, colours, dimension, outlining.

Plate VI in the colour section shows a Mind Map summarizing a 3-day Brain Training and Mind Mapping Course. The Mind Map was made by a father who was also a company director. He used the same Mind Map to summarize the course for himself, and to explain the course to his wife, children and business colleagues.

The central image refers to the integration of the brain and the body. The branches, moving clockwise from 'exercises' at 9 o'clock, summarize the major elements of the course.

Images, rather than words, provide succinct memory aids.

The Mind Map note of this three-day course, as you can see, is useful not only as a summary of all that was dealt with, but could also be used as the basis for a speech about the course.

In this situation the Mind Map becomes the 'note from your own brain' which then allows you to communicate to others, thus completing the speed and range reading cycle.

When used appropriately, the Mind Map will multiply your reading and learning efficiency by a factor of at least three, and will save massive amounts of time, thus increasing your overall reading effectiveness.

SUMMARY

1 The Mind Map is a powerful graphic technique which harnesses the full range of your cortical skills and unlocks the true potential of your brain.

2 The Mind Map can be applied to every aspect of your reading, studying and learning, and will enhance *all* levels of your performance.

HIGH EYE-CUE ACTION POINTS

1 As an interesting exercise, try 'reading' in detail the Mind Map on the Brain Training and Mind Mapping Course, to see how comprehensive a summary/understanding you can obtain from this one-page note.

2 Now that you have learnt the Mind Mapping technique, it will be useful for you to go back over the Self Tests in Chapters 1, 4, 6, 8 and 10 Continue to extract the key words from them, and to make Mind Maps of each essay. In this way you will be reviewing your speed reading skills, developing your note-taking and Mind Mapping techniques, and establishing basic knowledge foundations in the fields of the brain, psychology, art and science.

3 As you continue through *The Speed Reading Book*, make it a practice, after you have done each Self Test, to review it, underlining key words and concepts, and subsequently to Mind Map the article.

4 Finish this day's reading by thumbing through some of your old notes from school or other sources, observing how much was completely unnecessary, and how much time you could have saved, first in writing them down and second in reading them back. Many people find that only as little as 10 per cent was necessary. As you scan your notes and old books, make sure you are consistently using a guide and continuing with your acceleration training and exercises.

ONWORD
The next chapter will enable you to expand your knowledge of key words into a technique for analysing the structure of paragraphs. This will help to further increase your speed and comprehension.

CHAPTER FOURTEEN

Using Knowledge of Paragraph Structure to Increase Speed and Comprehension

By understanding the complexity of a part, you better understand the complexity of a whole. By understanding the complexity of a whole, you increase your ability to assimilate and understand everything.

FOREWORD
In Chapter 9 we discussed the process of skimming, in which certain pre-selected sections of the material are covered in order to gain a general overview. Here we shall discuss the **structure of the paragraph**, thus enabling you to put into practice your skimming techniques.

EXPLANATORY PARAGRAPHS
These are paragraphs in which the writer sets out to explain a certain concept or point of view. They will generally be quite easy to recognize, and should be fairly easy to understand. The first sentence or two of an explanatory paragraph will give you a general idea of what is going to be explained or discussed, the last sentence or two will contain the result or conclusion, and the middle of the paragraph will contain the details. Depending on your goal in reading you will, in the initial skimming, be able to direct your attention appropriately.

DESCRIPTIVE PARAGRAPHS
Descriptive paragraphs usually set the scene or expand on ideas that have been introduced previously. Such paragraphs usually embellish, and are therefore often less important than those that introduce main elements. Of course there are exceptions, in which the description of people or objects is vital, but in such cases you will usually be aware of this importance, and able to focus your attention appropriately.

LINKING PARAGRAPHS
These are paragraphs which join others together. As such, they often contain key information, because they tend to summarize the content of what has preceded and what follows. For example: 'The theory of evolution explained above will now be placed in the context of the latest developments in the field of biochemical genetic research.' In

this brief sentence we have been given an extraordinary amount of information, information that encapsulates the content of part of the material we are reading. Linking paragraphs, then, can be very useful as guides, and as tools for previewing and reviewing.

THE STRUCTURE AND POSITION OF PARAGRAPHS

How can you make use of the structure of paragraphs and their placing in the text to improve your reading efficiency?

The most important point is to realize that in newspaper and magazine articles the first and last few paragraphs usually contain most of the significant information, whereas the middle paragraphs tend to contain the details. If the material you are reading is of this type, concentrate, when skimming, on the opening and closing paragraphs.

Other writers 'clear their throats' at the beginning, before getting down to the meat of their presentation which is contained in the third or fourth paragraphs, and in such cases it is these on which you should concentrate initially.

There are two 'games' you can play with the structure of paragraphs which help enormously in understanding and maintaining involvement.

The first of these is to make up, as you read, a memory word for the main theme and the secondary theme of each paragraph. This exercise forces you to remain involved with the material and makes you think about it as you read it. Ultimately, you should aim to develop the ability to select these words as you read, without any pause or interruption to the flow of your reading.

It is possible, by using these key words, especially in Mind Map form, to memorize the details of an entire book. Indeed, the key memory words, in conjunction with images, will provide the basic building blocks of your Mind Map. (See *The Mind Map Book*.)

The second of these paragraph 'games' is to relate, as you read through the paragraph, the first sentence to the remainder, asking yourself whether this is introductory, transitional or encompassing, or whether, in fact, it has nothing to do with the words that follow it.

HIGH EYE-CUE ACTION POINTS

1 Do the first paragraph game on at least four different paragraphs.
2 Do the second paragraph game on at least four different paragraphs.
3 Using a guide, preview the next chapter.
4 Before moving on, read several different kinds of material to give yourself practice in the art of recognizing different paragraph types.

ONWORD

Knowing how to analyse paragraphs has given you analytical power over the material you read. The next chapter will give you an enhanced ability to see the whole picture.

CHAPTER FIFTEEN

Previewing – Your Mental Reconnaissance

Know the map if you wish to know the territory.

FOREWORD
We come, in this chapter, to a concept at which we have been hinting all along: **previewing** material before it is read. The purpose of the preview is to develop a structure into which the mind can more easily fit the smaller details of that structure, thus immediately improving your comprehension of the whole.

YOU AS YOUR OWN SCOUT
The previewer can be likened to a reconnaissance scout who goes ahead of the troops to determine the lie of the land, the position of the enemy forces, and areas of tactical advantage. It is easier for an army to manoeuvre and operate in unknown territory if it has major reference points; in the same way, it is easier for the mind to attack or understand information once it has major landmarks by which to go.

Previewing should be applied to whatever kind of material you are going to read, whether it be letters, reports, novels, or articles. In all cases, it will speed up your overall reading and will improve your understanding because you will no longer be stumbling over items one after the other, but will be fitting pieces into a general picture.

Your approach to the preview should combine the elements mentioned in Chapter 9 (on skimming) and Chapter 14 (on paragraph structure). In other words, you will sensibly and rapidly go over the material you are about to read, selecting those areas most likely to hold the major chunks of information. When you are previewing, *always* use your favourite guiding technique.

The concept of previewing as described here is for use in your general reading.

STRATEGIES FOR PREVIEWING
Playing the following 'Active Reading' games will guarantee that your mental set is more appropriate, that your cyclopean eye is searching for the best information as you preview, and that the whole process becomes more fun.

1 Apply What You Already Know

When you apply what you already know you will often find that you know more than you thought! Many people incorrectly assume that the author is the expert, when in fact very often the reader knows as much as or more than the author. Always quickly Mind Map your knowledge of the subject just before you read a new book. You can then use this knowledge to make new associations from the book, and to ask appropriate questions.

2 Interact Actively with the Author

When you read a book it should be a conversation between you and the brain that created the book; not a one-way lecture. It is most important that you interact with whatever text you read by noting down questions or comments in the margin of the book or on a separate piece of paper.

3 Be a Detective

Constantly try to predict what is going to happen next in the text, what 'plan of action' the author had. Keep trying to be one step ahead in solving the puzzle of the information you are absorbing.

SUMMARY

'Preview' means just what it says, when you break the word into its component parts: pre-view – to see before. When you allow your brain to see the whole text beforehand, you will navigate far more effectively on your second run-through.

HIGH EYE-CUE ACTION POINTS

1 Preview everything you read for the next two weeks, checking how much knowledge you gain from each preview, and how much more effectively it enables you to understand when you are reading the material for the second time.
2 Practise the previewing techniques you have learnt on a book, while at the same time using an advanced guiding technique to read the entire book in less than ten minutes.
3 Preview the next three chapters on developing your mastermind vocabulary.

ONWORD

One of the obstacles to effective speed reading is having a limited vocabulary. The next chapter shows you how to expand your knowledge of words beyond what you ever thought possible.

Developing Your Mastermind Vocabulary (I) *Prefixes*

The improvement of vocabulary is, historically, one of the most important factors in the raising of the level of human intelligences.

FOREWORD

Having dealt with the workings of the eye/brain system, the theory behind eye movements and the major problem areas in reading, we now move on to the first of three chapters on **vocabulary**. Chapter 16 introduces you to **three kinds of vocabulary** and lists **85 prefixes** which will give you access to the meanings of thousands of words.

THE IMPORTANCE OF VOCABULARY

The extent of one's vocabulary is an indication of the amount of material that one has been able to assimilate and read. Schools, colleges and universities therefore include general vocabulary testing as one of the major criteria by which they judge the suitability of applicants, and the success or failure of students often depends on their ability to understand and use words properly.

The importance of vocabulary extends, of course, far beyond the academic world: the businessman who has at his command a wider range of words than his peers is at an immediate advantage, and the person who, in social situations, can both understand easily and comment creatively also has the upper hand.

OUR THREE KINDS OF VOCABULARY

Most of us have more than one vocabulary. In fact we usually have at least three. First is the vocabulary we use in **conversation**, and in many cases this may not exceed 1000 words (it is estimated that the English language contains well over a million words).

Our second vocabulary is the one we use when **writing**. This tends to be larger than the spoken one, because more time is devoted to the construction and content of sentences, and because there is less pressure on the writer.

The largest of the three is our **recognition** vocabulary – the words that we understand and appreciate when we hear them in conversation or when we read them, but which we ourselves may not use either in writing or in conversation. Ideally, of course, both our speaking and our writing vocabulary should be as large as our recognition vocabulary, but in practice this is seldom the case. It is possible, however, to increase all three quite dramatically.

THE POWER OF PREFIXES

The purpose of this chapter is to introduce you to over 80 prefixes (letters, syllables or words placed at the beginning of a word). Many of them are concerned with position, opposition and movement. As the English language has a large element of Greek and Latin, many of the prefixes are from these two languages.

Just to give you some idea of the incredible power of these basic units of vocabulary, Dr Minninger, of the University of Minnesota, has estimated that 14 of these alone offer the keys to over 14,000 word meanings! She further confirms that, by the age of 25, the average person's vocabulary development has become almost moribund. It is 95 per cent complete, leaving a mere 5 per cent to be added over the possible 75 years of life that still remain. The 14 prefixes and roots listed below were found in over 14,000 words from a standard desk-top dictionary, and were found in *roughly 100,000 words* from a large unabridged dictionary.

These 'mini power words' have been extracted from the larger lists for you. As you read through this and the next two chapters, be on the look-out for them, as well as absorbing all the others.

14 Words Containing Key Prefixes

Words	Prefix	Common meaning	Roots	Common meaning
1 Precept	pre-	before	capere	take seize
2 Detain	de-	away, down	tenere	hold, have
3 Intermittent	inter-	between, among	mittere	send
4 Offer	ob-	against	ferre	bear, carry
5 Insist	in-	into	stare	stand
6 Monograph	mono-	alone, one	graphein	write
7 Epilogue	epi-	upon	logos	speech, study of
8 Aspect	ad-	to, toward	specere	see
9 Uncomplicated	un-	not	plicare	fold
	com-	together, with		
10 Non-extended	non-	not	tendere	stretch
	ex-	out, beyond		
11 Reproduction	re-	back, again	ducere	lead
	pro-	forward, for		
12 Indisposed	in-	not	ponere	put, place
	dis-	apart, not		

Words	Prefix	Common meaning	Roots	Common meaning
13 Over-sufficient	over-	above	facere	make, do
	sub-	under		
14 Mistranscribe	mis-	wrong	scribere	write
	trans-	across, beyond		

85 Prefixes

Study the following list thoroughly; it will give you the key to thousands of unfamiliar words. For a method of perfectly memorizing this list, and the lists in Chapters 17 and 18, refer to *Use Your Memory* by the author.

G = Greek, L = Latin, F = French, E = English

Prefix	Meaning	Example
a-, an- (G)	without, not	anaerobic
ab-, aabs- (L)	away, from, apart	absent
ad-, ac-, af- (L)	to, towards	advent, advance
aero-	air	aeroplane, aeronaut
amb-, ambi- (G)	both, around	ambiguous
amphi- (G)	both, around	amphitheatre
ante- (L)	before	antenatal
anti- (G)	against	antidote, anti-toxic
apo- (G)	away from	apostasy
arch- (G)	chief, most important	archbishop, arch-criminal
auto- (G)	self	automatic, autocrat
be-	about, make	belittle, beguile, beset
bene- (L)	well, good	benediction
bi- (G)	two	biennial, bicycle
by-, bye- (G)	added to	byways, bye-laws
cata- (G)	down	catalogue, cataract
centi-, cente- (L)	hundred	centigrade, centenary
circum- (L)	around	circumference, circumambient
co-, col-, com-, cor-	together	companion
con- (L)	with,	collect, co-operate
contra- (L)	against, counter	contradict, contraceptive
de- (F)	down	denude, decentralize
deca-, deci- (G)	ten	decade, decagon
demi- (L)	half	demigod
dia- (G)	through, between	diameter

Prefix	Meaning	Example
dis- (L)	not, opposite to	dislike, disagree
duo- (G)	two	duologue, duplex
dys- (G)	ill, hard	dysentry
e-, ex-	out of	exhale, excavate
ec- (L)	out of	eccentric
en-, in-, em-, im-, (L,G,F)	into, not	enrage, inability, emulate, impress
equi-	equally	equidistant
epi- (G)	upon, at, in addition	epidemic, epidermis
extra- (L)	outside, beyond	extra-essential
for-, fore- (E)	before	foresee
hemi- (G)	half	hemisphere
hepta- (G)	seven	heptagon
hexa- (G)	six	hexagon, hexateuch
homo- (L)	same	homonym
hyper- (G)	above, excessive	hypercritical, hypertrophy
il-	not	illegal, illogical
in-, im-, (un) (L, G, F)	not	imperfect, inaccessible
inter- (L)	among, between	interrupt, intermarriage
intra-, intro- (L)	inside, within	intramural, introvert
iso- (G)	equal, same	isobaric, isosceles
mal- (L)	bad, wrong	malfunction, malformed
meta- (G)	after, beyond	metabolism, metaphysical
mis-	wrongly	misfit, mislead
mono- (G)	one, single	monotonous, monocular
multi- (L)	many	multipurpose, multimillion
non-	not	nonsense, nonpareil
ob-, oc-, of-, op- (L)	in the way of, resistance	obstruct, obstacle, oppose
octa-, octo- (G)	eight	octahedron, octave
off-	away, apart	offset
out-	beyond	outnumber, outstanding
over-	above	overhear, overcharge
para- (G)	aside, beyond	parable, paradox
penta- (G)	five	pentagon, pentateuch
per- (L)	through	perennial, peradventure
peri- (G)	around, about	perimeter, pericardium

Prefix	Meaning	Example
poly- (G)	many	polygamy, polytechnic
post- (L)	after	postscript, post-natal
pre- (L)	before	prehistoric, pre-war
prime, primo- (L)	first, important	primary, prime minister
pro- (L)	in front of, favouring	pronoun, protect
quadri-	four	quadrennial, quadrangle
re- (L)	again, back	reappear, recivilize
retro- (L)	backward	retrograde, retrospect
se-	aside	secede
self-	personalizing	self-control, self-taught
semi- (G)	half	semi-circle, semi-detached
sub- (L)	under	submarine, subterranean
super- (L)	above, over	superfluous, superior
syl-	with, together	syllogism
syn-, sym (G)	together	sympathy, synchronize
tele- (G)	far, at or to a distance	telegram, telepathy
ter- (L)	three times	tercentenary
tetra- (G)	four	tetrahedron, tetralogy
trans- (L)	across, through	transatlantic, translate
tri- (L,G)	three	triangle, tripartite
ultra- (L)	beyond	ultramarine, ultra-violet
un- (im) (L, G, F)	not	unbroken, unbutton, unable
under-	below	underfed, underling
uni- (L)	one	unicellular, uniform
vice- (L)	in place of	viceroy, vice-president
yester- (E)	preceding time	yesterday, yesteryear

SUMMARY
1 The average person's conversational vocabulary is about a thousand words; the number of available words is over a million.
2 Of our three vocabularies (conversational, written and recognition), recognition is the largest.
3 Improving your vocabulary raises your intelligence.
4 Just learning a few prefixes can expand your vocabulary by leaps and bounds.

HIGH EYE-CUE VOCABULARY MASTERMIND EXERCISES
The following exercises are not vocabulary tests in the strict sense. In many cases definitions have been 'stretched' a little in

order to include a key word that carries an appropriate prefix.

At the top of each vocabulary exercise there are 15 words, from which you can choose the correct answer to each of the 15 questions.

When doing this exercise break up each of the words you select into its component parts, trying to establish its meaning from its structure. To help you with this, have a dictionary at hand.

When you have filled in each of the 15 blank spaces with the letter of the word you think is correct, check your answers on page 186.

Vocabulary 1 (a)

a. polyglot *b. amphibian* *c. disenchantment* *d. centipede* *e. biped*
f. confluent *g. illiterate* *h. antipathetic* *i. retroactive* *j. contravene*
k. tertiary *l. arch-enemy* *m. paragon* *n. triumvirate* *o. impregnation*

1 The most important and most dangerous of one's opponents is one's ....

2 A .... is a two-footed animal.

3 A person or thing beyond comparison, a model of excellence, is known as a ....

4 Streams that flow together are said to be ....

5 A coalition of three men for the purposes of government or administration is called a ....

6 Many people in the world are not able to read; they are ....

7 .... is the introduction of one substance into another.

8 Because people estimated that this creature had 100 legs, they called it a ....

9 .... means third in rank, order or succession.

10 One opposite of fascination is ....

11 To go against restrictions laid down is to .... the rules.

12 A creature that can live in both air and water is called an ....

13 .... means operating in a backward direction.

14 A .... is a person who speaks many languages.

15 If you have a strong feeling against something you are said to be ....

Vocabulary 1 (b)

*a. intravenous b. autobiographer c. abdicates d. Decalogue
e. atheist f. undermine g. supercilious h. isotherm i. monomaniac
j. octagon k. catacomb l. obfuscate m. periscope n. prominent
o. heminaopsia*

1 Someone who does not believe in God is an ....

2 He was a .... because he had a fixation on a single object.

3 The Ten Commandments are often called the ....

4 An outstanding object or person is said to be ....

5 A plane figure with eight sides and angles is known as an ....

6 To .... means to dig away the foundations, to bring down from below.

7 A .... is a graveyard below ground.

8 A person who .... gives up a claim, resigns, gets away from a situation.

9 An injection into the returning bloodstream is called an .... injection.

10 When something gets in the way of light or meaning, it is said to . ...

11 To consider oneself to be above others is to possess a .... attitude.

12 The medical condition in which one loses one half of one's field of vision is known as ....

13 A .... is an instrument that enables observers to look over an object.

14 A line on a map which connects those places having equal average temperature is called an ....

15 An .... is a person who writes his own life story.

Vocabulary 1 (c)

*a. metaphysical b. regurgitate c. forebear d. extravagate
e. misconstrue f. primordial g. circumspect h. diaphragm
i. subjugate j. predeterminable k. nonentity l. pentameter
m. beneficence n. pervade o. malediction*

1 A dividing membrane between two areas is called a ....

2 .... applies to what is immaterial, incorporeal, super-sensory, beyond the physical.

3 A .... is a curse.

4 To .... means to bring up or throw back from a deep place; to vomit.

5 A .... is someone who is of no importance.

6 An ancestor may also be called a ....

7 When something passes through, permeates, extends and is diffused, it is said to ....

8 If you .... you are going beyond ordinary limits.

9 A verse containing five feet is called a ....

10 .... is charity, kindness or generosity.

11 If you are prudent and wary, and look all around before doing anything you are ....

12 Something capable of being calculated beforehand is ....

13 That which has existed from the beginning, we call ....

14 To .... means to subdue by superior force; to bring under the yoke.

15 If we interpret something wrongly, we .... it.

Prefix Detective Exercise

With your new knowledge of prefixes, read through any part of *The Speed Reading Book* that you have already completed, and underline all the prefixes you can. You will find that they pop up at least once in almost every hundred words you read. Repeat this same exercise at the end of the next two chapters, adding first suffixes and finally roots, especially concentrating on the 14 key power words.

ONWORD

Having 'topped' tens of thousands of words with prefixes, you can now move on to 'tail' them with suffixes. Be on the look-out for the 14 key prefixes.

CHAPTER SEVENTEEN

Developing Your Mastermind Vocabulary (II) *Suffixes*

The use of increasingly complex and sophisticated language structures, and the units (vocabulary) that make up those structures, is one of the defining characteristics of evolutionary development. The nurturing and training of your skill in this area is your natural right, your own responsibility, and a rare opportunity which, if grasped, will provide you with exceptional benefits. Claim it. Accept it. Do it.

FOREWORD
At the end of Chapter 16, you were introduced to 86 prefixes which were then tested. By now your facility with this building block of vocabulary, especially if you have used the information you have so far gathered from *The Speed Reading Book,* will have increased considerably and you will be ready for the next step in vocabulary building. This is to learn the **suffixes** (the letters, syllables, or words placed at the end of words). As in the section on prefixes you will notice that most suffixes are taken from the Latin and the Greek.

THE POWER OF SUFFIXES
This chapter introduces you to 51 suffixes, many of which are concerned with characteristics or qualities, or changing one part of speech into another (e.g. adjectives into adverbs).

51 Suffixes

G = Greek, L = Latin, F = French, E = English

Suffix	Meaning	Example
-able, -ible (L)	capable of, fit for	durable, comprehensible
-acy (L,G)	state or quality of	accuracy
-age (L)	action or state of	breakage
-al, -ial (L)	relating to	abdominal
-an (-ane, -ian) (L)	the nature of	Grecian, African
-ance, -ence	quality or actions of	insurance, corpulence
-ant (L)	forming adjectives of quality, and nouns signifying a personal agent or something producing an effect	defiant, servant

142

Suffix	Meaning	Example
stable (L)	(see -able, -ible)	
-arium, -orium (L)	place for	aquarium, auditorium
-ary (L)	place for, dealing with	seminary, dictionary
-ate (L)	cause to be, office of	animate, magistrate
-ation, -ition (L)	action or state of	condition, dilapidation
-cle, -icle (L)	diminutive	icicle
-dom (E)	condition or control	kingdom
-en (E)	small	mitten
-en (E)	quality	golden, broken
-er (E)	belonging to	farmer, New Yorker
-ess (E)	feminine suffix	hostess, waitress
-et, -ette (L)	small	puppet, marionette
-ferous (L)	producing	coniferous
-ful (E)	full of	colourful, beautiful
-fy, -ify (L)	make	satisfy, fortify
-hood (E)	state or condition of	boyhood, childhood
-ia (L)	names of classes, names of places	bacteria, America
-ian (L)	practitioners or inhabitants	musician, Parisian
-ion (L)	condition or action of	persuasion
-ic (G)	relating to	historic
-id(e) (L)	a quality	acid
-ine (G,L)	a compound	chlorine
-ish (E)	a similarity or relationship	childish, greenish
-ism (G)	quality or doctrine of	realism, socialism
-itis (L)	inflammation of (medical)	bronchitis
-ist (G)	one who practises	chemist, pessimist
-ity, -ety, ty (L)	state or quality of	loyalty
-ive (L)	nature of	creative, receptive
-ize, -ise (G)	make, practise, act like	modernize, advertise
-less (E)	lacking	fearless, faceless
-logy (G)	indicating a branch of knowledge	biology, psychology
-lent (L)	fullness	violent
-ly (E)	having the quality of	softly, quickly
-ment (L)	act or condition of	resentment
-metry, -meter (G)	measurement	gasometer, geometry
-mony	resulting condition	testimony
-oid (G)	resembling	ovoid
-or (L)	a state of action, a person who, or thing which	error, governor, victor, generator

Suffix	Meaning	Example
-ous, -ose (L)	full of	murderous, anxious, officious, morose
-osis	process or condition of	metamorphosis
-some	like	gladsome
-tude	quality or degree of	altitude, gratitude
-ward (E)	direction	backward, outward
-y (E)	condition	difficulty

HIGH EYE-CUE VOCABULARY MASTERMIND EXERCISES

Vocabulary 2 (a)

a. indefatigable *b.* vignette *c.* demobilize *d.* epididymitis *e.* practitioner
f. ignominy *g.* supremacy *h.* platitude *i.* untoward *j.* cursive
k. chauvinist *l.* prioress *m.* hedonism *n.* embolden *o.* bondage

1 .... is the condition of being marked with disgrace.

2 A .... is a woman who governs a nunnery.

3 Someone who has very strong nationalistic feelings and who makes a practice of this somewhat exaggerated patriotism is called a ....

4 That which is intractable, unruly, perverse; which goes in the wrong unpredictable direction is ....

5 A .... is one who works in a certain field, such as medicine.

6 A ....is a comment or statement which is insipid and trite.

7 The unpleasant medical condition in which part of the testicle becomes irritated and inflamed is known as ....

8 To .... is to imbue with the added qualities of courage, inspiration and fearlessness.

9 The doctrine of pursuing pleasure as the highest good is known as ....

10 If you are capable of working 12 hours a day without a rest; if you can engage in physical exercise for hours without seeming to get tired, then you are ....

11 Handwriting which is in the nature of a running hand; which forms the character rapidly without raising the pen is known as................. handwriting.

12 A .... is a small ornamental design, drawing or picture.

13 The quality or state of being uppermost, of having complete authority or power, is the state of ....

14 To .... is to render something unable to operate or move; to disband.

15 .... is the state of being bound or tied to something, either physically or mentally.

Vocabulary 2 (b)
a. winsome b. minimal c. irritant d. enervation e. vociferous
f. bellicose g. aviary h. corpuscle i. magnate j. hoydenish
k. baleful l. placid m. osmosis n. planetarium o. martyrdom

1 Someone who places himself in a condition of suffering for his beliefs, is placing himself in a position of ....

2 A diminutive particle of matter is sometimes known as a ...., although this term now usually applies to the small particles constituting blood.

3 A girl who is joyful, attractive and engaging is ....

4 A charge for something which relates to the lowest or smallest price is ....

5 .... is the process in which fluids tend to mix, even through porous membranes.

6 A .... is a place where one goes to see models or projections of the solar system and other parts of the universe.

7 People who speak loudly and often are ....

8 .... is the state of being exhausted.

9 A rude girl or tomboy is said to be ....

10 A .... person is full of antagonism and the desire to quarrel or fight.

11 A place where birds are kept is known as an ....

12 A .... look is one full of mischief or malice.

13 A .... is a person who holds high rank or status.

14 To be gentle, quiet, peaceful and serene is to be ....

15 An .... is that which provokes or produces discomfort or inflammation.

Vocabulary 2 (c)
a. mundane b. narcissistically c. intelligentsia d. insatiable e. intensify
f. rhetorician g. deity h. psychology i. physiology j. pestilence
k. hardihood l. annulment m. anthropoid n. metabolic o. indolent

1 To be filled with the desire to do nothing, to be lazy, phlegmatic and idle is to be ....

2 A .... is an eloquent speaker or writer.

3 The .... is that class of educated people who tend to form much of public opinion.

4 .... relates or pertains to the constant chemical changes in living matter.

5 An .... is any creature which resembles man.

6 The branch of knowledge which deals with the body's organs and their functions is ....

7 A synonym for a state of boldness, courage and robustness is ....

8 That which is 'of the nature of the world' is often said to be ....

9 A disease, the qualities of which are plague-like and virulent, is often called a ....

10 .... is the act of having a contract or marriage abolished.

11 To look at oneself .... is to have the quality of the vain god who fell in love with his reflected image.

12 To .... is to raise to a higher or more extreme degree.

13 When we attribute divine qualities to someone or something we make him or it a ....

14 Someone whose appetites cannot be satisfied is ....

15 The branch of knowledge which deals with the human mind and its functioning is ....

Suffix Expansion Exercise
After completing the vocabulary tests to your satisfaction, browse through a good dictionary studying the various ways in which these suffixes are used. Keep a record of exceptionally good examples or examples which you find interesting and useful.

ONWORD
Now that you have learnt the beginnings and endings of modern English words, you can move on to roots, those elements from Latin and Greek that can be found anywhere in a modern word.

CHAPTER EIGHTEEN

Developing Your Mastermind Vocabulary (III) *Roots*

The pen is mightier than the sword only if the brain behind it knows how to wield the word.

FOREWORD

Chapter 18, the last of the vocabulary chapters, deals with Latin and Greek **roots** (words from which others are derived) and also suggests **five steps for continuing your vocabulary development.**

FIVE STEPS FOR CONTINUING YOUR MASTERMIND VOCABULARY IMPROVEMENT

As this is the last chapter dealing with words and their meanings, I should like to offer a few hints on how you can continue to improve your vocabulary.

First, perform the exercise described in Chapter 17; that is, browse through a good dictionary, studying the various ways in which the prefixes, suffixes and roots you have learnt are used. Keep a record of noteworthy examples and useful words. (If you own one, keep this record in the creative development section of the Universal Personal Organizer (UPO) Buzan Diary system.)

Second, make a continuing and concentrated effort to introduce into your vocabulary at least one new word a day. New words are only retained if they are repeated a number of times; so, once you have selected your word or words, make sure you use them often and effectively.

Third, be on the look-out for new and exciting words in conversations. If you are embarrassed about asking a speaker to define his terminology, make a quick mental note or jot the word down and look it up later.

Fourth, keep an eagle eye out for unfamiliar words in anything you read. *Don't* write them down as you read, but make a mark with a pencil and look them up afterwards.

And **finally**, if you feel so inclined, go to your local bookshop or library and ask for a book on vocabulary training – there are a number and most of them are quite helpful.

147

51 Roots

Root	Meaning	Example
aer	air	aerate, aeroplane
am (from *amare*)	love	amorous, amateur, amiable
ann (from *annus*)	year	annual, anniversary
aud (from *audire*)	hear	auditorium, audit
bio	life	biography
cap (from *capire*)	take	captive
cap (from *caput*)	head	capital, per capita, decapitate
chron	time	chronology, chronic
cor	heart	cordial
corp	body	corporation
de	god	deify, deity
dic, dict	say, speak	dictate
duc (from *ducere*)	lead	aqueduct, duke, ductile
ego	I	egotism
equi	equal	equidistant
fac, fic (from *facere*)	make, do	manufacture, efficient
frat	brother	fraternity
geo	earth	geology
graph	write	calligraphy, graphology, telegraph
loc (from *locus)*	place	location, local
loqu, loc (from *loqui)*	speak	eloquence, circumlocution
luc (from *lux)*	light	elucidate
man (from *manus)*	hand	manuscript, manipulate
mit, miss (from *mittere)*	send	admit, permission
mort (from *mors)*	death	immortal
omni	all	omnipotent, omnibus
pat (from *pater)*	father	paternal
path	suffering, feeling	sympathy, pathology
ped (from *pes)*	foot	impede, millipede, pedal
photo	light	photography
phobia, phobe	fear	hydrophobe, xenophobia
pneum	air, breath, spirit	pneumonia
pos, posit	place	deposit, position
pot, poss, poten (from *ponerte)*	be able	potential, possible
quaerere	ask, question, seek	inquiry, query
rog (from *rogare)*	ask	interrogate
scrib, scrip (from *scribere)*	write	scribble, script, inscribe
sent, sens (from *sentire)*	feel	sensitive, sentient
sol	alone	soloist, isolate

Root	Meaning	Example
soph	wise	philosopher
spect (from spicere)	look	introspective, inspect
spir (from spirare)	breathe	inspiration
therm (from thermos)	warm	thermometer
ten (from tendere)	stretch	extend, tense
ten (from tenere)	hold	tenant
utilis	useful	utility
ven, vent (from venire)	come, arrive	advent, convenient
vert, vers (from vertere)	turn	revert, adverse
vid, vis (from videre)	see	supervisor, vision, provident

Vocabulary 3 (a)

a. expire b. translucent c. audition d. sophist e. annuity
f. agoraphobia g. querulous h. amiable i. thermal j. dislocated
k. graphology l. impotent m. telepathy n. soliloquy o. homologous

1 A person who is friendly and lovable is often described as ....

2 A .... is a wise or would-be learned man.

3 Material through which light can travel is ....

4 You are .... if you are unable to perform or act.

5 An .... is a payment made yearly.

6 When an actor stands alone on a stage and speaks to himself his speech is known as a ....

7 The word ...., which now usually means to pass away or die, derives from the idea of breathing out.

8 If a bone is out of joint, or misplaced, we say it is ....

9 The transference of thoughts from one mind to another over a distance is known as ....

10 .... means to be alike in proportion, value or structure; to be in a corresponding position.

11 A person who is quarrelsome and discontented, and who complains in a questioning manner is ....

12 .... means pertaining to heat.

13 A trial hearing of an applicant for employment, especially in the case of actors and singers, is known as an ....

14 .... is the controversial art of analysing personality from handwriting.

15 If you suffer from a fear of open spaces, you suffer from ....

Vocabulary 3 (b)

*a. tendentious b. artefact c. convene d. decapitate e. corporeal
f. manciple g. equinox h. captivate i. abduction j. egocentric
k. geomorphology l. omniscient m. interdict n. utilitarian
o. patricide*

1 If you behead someone you .... him.

2 A .... argument is one that stretches the truth in order to convince.

3 .... is the study of the physical features of the crust of the Earth.

4 To .... is to take complete control of the attention; to overcome by charm of manner and appearance.

5 A person who considers himself to be the centre of the universe is described as ....

6 ...., a term usually reserved for God, is occasionally applied to people who seem to know everything.

7 A .... is someone who holds that actions are right only if they are useful.

8 An .... is a statement which comes between a person and his intended action; a prohibition.

9 The murder of one's own father is known as ....

10 If something is made by, or results from art; if it is in some way artificial, we say it is an ....

11 The .... is that time of year when both day and night are of equal length.

12 A .... is a steward or servant (someone who waits on you hand and foot!).

13 .... means to cause to come together; to call to an assembly.

14 That which has a material body is said to be ....

15 .... is leading or carrying away, usually by fraud or force.

Vocabulary 3 (c)

a. chronometer *b.* imposition *c.* subrogation *d.* elucidate
e. insensate *f.* desolation *g.* morbid *h.* vertigo *i.* remittance
j. fraternize *k.* empathy *l.* pneumatic *m.* bioplasm *n.* aerodynamics
o. tenacious

1 A person who is destitute of sense or given to extremes, we call
....

2 .... is the power to project one's feelings into an object
or person, and so reach full understanding.

3 .... means to shed light on, to make clear.

4 A .... drill is one that uses compressed air.

5 An instrument that finely measures time is a ....

6 A .... person is one who holds on, no matter what the
circumstances.

7 A .... is money sent to you.

8 The science which deals with the forces exerted by air and by
gaseous fluids is ....

9 The germinal matter for all living things is ....

10 When people associate as brothers, we say they ....

11 If something is .... it reminds us of death.

12 An .... may be defined as the act of placing or putting
on; a burden, often unwelcome.

13 .... is when you substitute someone else for yourself
in respect of your legal rights.

14 .... refers to that which is deserted, laid waste,
solitary, forsaken.

15 .... is a feeling of giddiness.

DIVISION SUMMARY

In this division we have concentrated on establishing the basic building blocks of your intellect, by learning how to Mind Map, and how to
use the knowledge of paragraph structure in conjunction with
previewing techniques to enhance your reading speed and comprehension even further.

The three chapters on developing your vocabulary guarantee that
your overall intellect will improve, and that your understanding and
comprehension will increase considerably. Your reading speed will

also accelerate because of your increased comprehension, your enhanced ability to spot key words and concepts, and the fact that your increasingly powerful vocabulary will eliminate any need for back-skipping and regression.

ONWORD
You now possess all the basic knowledge about your eyes, your brain, and about fundamental learning techniques. You are therefore ready to move on to advanced techniques that will enable you to study more effectively, to gain control of the growing piles of magazines, newspapers and memos, to deal with electronic information, to appreciate more fully fine literature (including novels and poetry), to create your own growing knowledge library, and to look into your extraordinary abilities for the future. These are all covered in **Division 5 – Becoming a Master Reader: Advanced Use of Your Eye/Brain Systems**.

Since 1966 I have taught the fundamental principles of speed and range reading in more than 50 countries, to students ranging from three-year-old children to chief executives of multinational corporations. In every country, for every age, and no matter what the individual's position, similar questions arise concerning the application of the theory to the actual process of reading. These questions include:

'I can see how you would use this for other subjects, but you couldn't really use it for the sciences, could you?'

'You wouldn't apply speed and range reading to the appreciation of literature and poetry would you?'

'You surely wouldn't preview a detective story!'

'On really difficult material, you'd have to read slowly, wouldn't you?'

'Surely you wouldn't use speed and range reading if you were reading for relaxation and pleasure?'

'But I read to help me get to sleep – how can I use these techniques to help me do that!?'

Intriguingly, the answer is that your growing knowledge of how to read can be applied to *all* the aforementioned situations. What you have been learning and will continue to learn throughout the pages of *The Speed Reading Book* is an entire range of reading skills from which you can pick the appropriate individual items or combinations of items to fit your particular reading task/goal.

From now on, every page of every book you read will be approached slightly differently from every other page, and you will be to the printed word as a dolphin is to water.

The chapters in this division give you more detailed information on advanced applications, using the new information on your eye/brain system, and introduce you to the revolutionary new concept of the Knowledge File.

CHAPTER NINETEEN

The Mind Map Organic Study Technique (MMOST)

*It has been said that knowledge is power. In truth, power lies in the ability to assimilate, comprehend, understand, retain, recall, communicate, and the consequent ability to create new knowledge from your extant multidimensional mental encyclopaedia. The key to this power is **learning how to learn**.*

FOREWORD
This chapter introduces you to the **Mind Map Organic Study Technique**, a unique powerful tool for learning.

THE MIND MAP ORGANIC STUDY TECHNIQUE
Study reading is an area to which all the techniques contained in this book can be applied. During the nineteenth century, educationalists gradually realized that multi-level reading for study purposes was far more effective than simply reading the book once through, and they devised several different systems. The MMOST technique incorporates the main elements of these previous learning techniques, as well as all the brain-compatible skills, including Mind Mapping, the memory principles and systems, and the speed reading processes. MMOST is explained in full in *The Mind Map Book* but, very briefly, the technique is divided into two parts, preparation and application, which are explained below.

I Preparation

(a) Browse
Use the previewing skills taught in Chapter 15 to gain a 'bird's eye' view of the text.

(b) Time and amount
Set the time periods and the quantities of material to be covered in these periods. (See Fig.14, opposite and Fig.15, page 156.)

(c) Previous knowledge Mind Map
Using a Mind Map, search your memory for previous knowledge on the topic, thus ensuring that you have an appropriate mental set.

(d) Goals and objectives'
Establish clearly why you are reading the material and what you want to get out of it.

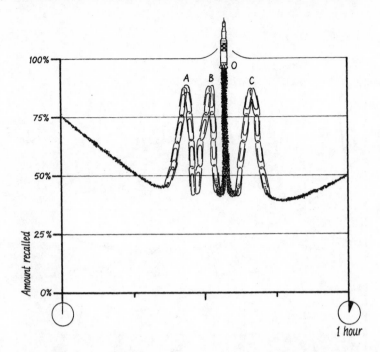

Fig. 14 Graph showing that we recall more from the beginning and end of a learning period. We also recall more when things are associated or linked (A, B and C) and more when things are outstanding or unique (O).

II Application

(a) Overview
Do a second and 'deeper' browse, using your goals and questions to select appropriate foundation information.

(b) Preview
Having established the basic structure of the information, begin to zoom in on the relevant parts, focusing on beginnings and endings.

(c) Inview
Fill in the bulk of the remaining information and build up your Mind Map, leaving difficult areas for the final stage.

(d) Review
The final integration. Complete your Mind Map, solve any remaining problems, answer remaining questions and complete all your goals.

You are approaching the end of the Self Tests! Before completing Self Test 6, increase your motivation, practise acceleration exercises

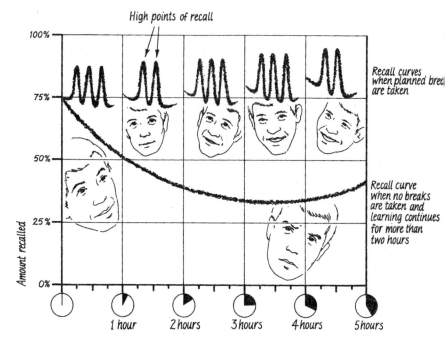

Fig. 15 Recall during learning – with and without breaks. A learning period of between 20–50 minutes produces the best relationship between understanding and recall.

with your guide, make sure you are holding the book a good distance from you, preview well, and use relevant information from the MMOST technique to help you increase your speed and comprehension even further.

SELF TEST 6 The Awakening Earth: Our Next Evolutionary Leap – The Global Brain
by Peter Russell

It is commonplace today to speak of the pace of life speeding up, and to look back with nostalgia at the more leisurely pace of our grandparents. But a brief look at the history of evolution reveals that this speeding up is not new; it has been going on since the universe began, some 15 billion years ago. Since billions of years are beyond our experience it may be difficult to appreciate this acceleration. We can get a more tangible image if we compress these 15 billion years into a film a year long – the ultimate epic!

The 'Big Bang', with which the film opens, is over in a fraction of a second – the universe 'created' in the first second of the first day of this New Year! The first atoms are formed about 25 minutes after you have sung 'Auld Lang Syne'! No more significant changes happen during the rest of the first day, nor for the rest of January (you will need plenty of popcorn): all that you are viewing is an expanding cloud of gas. Around February and March the gas clouds begin slowly condensing into clusters of galaxies and stars. As the weeks and months pass by, stars occasionally explode in supernovae, new stars condensing from the debris. Our own sun and solar system are eventually formed in early September – after eight months of film.

Once the Earth has formed, things begin to move a little faster as complex molecules start to take shape. Within two weeks, by the beginning of October, simple algae and bacteria appear. Then comes a relative lull (and more popcorn!) while the bacteria slowly evolve, developing photosynthesis a week later. In mid-November, complex cells with well-defined nuclei evolve, making sexual reproduction possible, and with this stage accomplished, evolution accelerates again. It is now late November, and the major part of the film has been seen. The evolution of life, however, has only just begun.

The first simple multi-cellular organisms appear around early December. The first vertebrates crawl out of the sea onto the land a week or so later. Dinosaurs rule the land for most of the last week of the film, from Christmas to midday on 30 December – a long and noble reign!

Our early ape-like (or dolphin-like?!) ancestors make their debut around the middle of the last day, but not until 11 o'clock in the evening do they walk upright.

Now, on New Year's Eve of the year which is just now beginning and after 365 days and nights of film, we come to some of the most fascinating developments. Human language begins to develop one and a half minutes before midnight. In the last half minute farming begins. Buddha achieves enlightenment under the bodhi tree five and a half seconds before the end, and Christ appears a second later. The Industrial Revolution occurs in the last half second, and World War II occurs less than a tenth of a second before midnight.

We are down to the last frame now, the last inch of a hundred thousand miles of film. The rest of modern history happens in a flash, not much longer than the flash with which the film started. Moreover, evolution is continuing to accelerate, and this rapid acceleration shows no signs of abating.

The rate of change in many areas of activity is now so fast that it is difficult to predict where we will be in 50 years' time, let alone have any idea of civilization in a thousand or a million years. It is becoming increasingly difficult to avoid the conclusion that we who are alive today truly are at a unique point in evolution.

In some respects humanity is beginning to behave like a planetary nervous system, and we find a close parallel between the phases of development of the young human brain and what is happening to humanity.

In 1980 the worldwide telecommunications network consisted of 440 million telephones, and nearly one million telex machines. Yet this network, intricate as it might seem, represents only a minute fraction of the communication terminals in the brain, the *trillions* of synapses through which nerve cells interact. According to John McNulty, a British computer consultant, the global telecommunications network of 1975 was no more complex than a region of the brain less than the size of a pea. But overall data-processing capacity is doubling every two and a half years, and if this rate of increase is sustained the global telecommunications network could equal the brain in complexity by the year 2000 – if this seems an unbelievably short time ahead, consider the acceleration during the last hour before midnight in our year-long film, and multiply that acceleration of change by the number of hours between midnight on 1 January 1997 and the New Year's Eve that will take us into the twenty-first century.

The changes which this will bring will be so great that their full impact will probably boggle even the imaginations of our infinite brains! No longer will we perceive ourselves as isolated individuals; *we will know ourselves to be part of a rapidly integrating global network, the nerve cells of an awakening global brain.* Yet, although this may be a possible direction for humanity, it is also very clear that the species is in a state of severe crisis, and will need to act purposefully and imaginatively in order to make it to the next century. We are deeply entangled in the most complex web of social, political, economic, ecological and moral crises in human history. Will these crises forestall an evolutionary leap? Perhaps. Certainly we have any number of doomsday projections which explore the possibilities of apocalypse in detail, but the history of evolution reveals quite another possible scenario – that *crises may be an evolutionary catalyst in the push towards higher order.*

Let's take a look at some of the major crises in evolution, and see how what may have appeared to be 'negative' was in fact highly positive in evolutionary terms.

One early crisis in the evolution of life probably occurred when the simple organic compounds on which the first primitive cells fed started running short. There was, in effect, a food crisis. The response was the evolution of photosynthesis – the ability to feed directly from sunlight. Photosynthesis, however, produced oxygen as a by-product, and although we live quite happily in it today, it spelt death to the creatures of the time.

One and a half billion years later, as the oxygen began to build up in the atmosphere, there was another major crisis, this time of pollution and poison. Evolution's response was the evolution of oxygen-breathing cells. Initially, any crisis looks painful and dangerous. Imagine what a committee of bacteria would have said about the environmental impact of a small group of bacteria's plans to use photosynthesis: 'The oxygen produced by this process is dangerous stuff. It is poisonous to all known forms of life and it is also highly inflammable, likely to burn us all to ashes. It is almost certain to lead to the destruction of life.'

Without doubt photosynthesis would have been banned as 'selfish, unnatural and irresponsible'. Luckily for us, no such committee existed, and photosynthesis went ahead. It did indeed bring about a major crisis, but on the other side of it came plants, animals, you and me.

Our present set of global problems may turn out to be of equal importance to our continued evolution as was the oxygen crisis. Never in the history of the human race have the dangers been so extreme, and we seem to be rapidly approaching the critical point. The result will be either breakdown or breakthrough. In their role as evolutionary catalysts, the crises may be just what is needed to push us to a higher level.

The idea that crises have both negative and positive aspects is captured in a word the Chinese have for crisis: *wei-chi*. The first part of the word means 'beware, danger'. The second part, however, has a very different implication. It means 'opportunity for change'.

The concept of *wei-chi* allows us to appreciate the importance of both aspects of crisis. In recent years, our attention has generally been focused on the *'wei'*, on the many possibilities for global catastrophe and how to avoid them. This will continue to be necessary as we strive to deal with the very real problems that face us. At the same time, we can find ourselves questioning some of our basic attitudes and values: Why are we here? What do we really want? Isn't there more to life? This questioning opens us up to the other aspect of crisis – the opportunity to change direction, to benefit from the prodigious and breathtaking opportunities that could be before us.

If we do not make the transition it may be thousands of years before humanity stands upon the threshold again. Or it may never happen with the human species. If we wipe ourselves out it may take millions of years for another species to evolve with the same potential. It may not even happen on this planet; but there may be plenty of other planets in our galaxy, and plenty in other galaxies. The universe will carry on evolving towards higher levels of integration and complexity whether we do or not.

If, on the other hand, humanity does find ways to resolve the various problems and conflicts facing it, it will have proved it can adapt successfully. In this respect *crises serve both as evolutionary catalysts, and as evolutionary tests*, examining the adaptability and viability of the system.

Humanity's currently growing set of crises could well be seen in this light: we may have reached the final test of our viability for further evolution.

Moreover, this test has a time limit. We do not have aeons to experiment; *it is we who are alive today who must answer these questions in order to save ourselves in the ongoing evolutionary process.*

Whether or not we pass is up to us. If we do pass, we may well move through into our next evolutionary phase. The task of showing whether or not humanity is viable rests with us – each one of us. Unlike other species in the past, humanity, with its incredible brain power, can anticipate the future, make conscious choices and deliberately change its own destiny. For the first time in the whole history of evolution, responsibility for the continued unfoldment of evolution has been placed upon the evolutionary material itself. We are no longer passive witnesses to the process – we *can* actively shape the future. We are now the custodians of the evolutionary process on Earth. Within our own hands – or rather, within our own brains and minds – lies the evolutionary future of this planet.

* *

Stop Your Timer Now
Length of time: .... mins

Next calculate your reading speed in words per minute (wpm) by simply dividing the number of words in the passage (in this case 1802) by the time (in minutes) you took.

Speed Reading Formula:

$$\text{words per minute (wpm)} = \frac{\text{number of words}}{\text{time}}$$

When you have completed your calculation, enter the number in the wpm slot at the end of this paragraph, and enter it on your Progress Chart and your Progress Graph on page 187.

Words per minute: ....

SELF TEST 6: COMPREHENSION

1 The universe began some:
(a) 5 million
(b) 75 million
(c) 12 billion
(d) 15 billion
years ago

2 In Russell's 'one-year universe' gas clouds begin slowly condensing into clusters of galaxies and stars in:
(a) January/February
(b) February/March
(c) March/April
(d) April/May

3 In Russell's 'one-year universe' our own sun and solar system are eventually formed in early:
(a) July
(b) August
(c) September
(d) October

4 In Russell's 'one-year universe' simple algae and bacteria appear:
(a) by the beginning of September
(b) by the beginning of October
(c) by the beginning of November
(d) by the beginning of December

5 In Russell's 'one-year universe' our ape-like ancestors walk upright in:
(a) October
(b) November
(c) the last two weeks
(d) the last hour of the last day

6 In Russell's 'one-year universe' human language begins to develop:
(a) during the last two weeks
(b) during the last week
(c) at the beginning of the last hour
(d) one and a half minutes before midnight

7 In Russell's 'one-year universe' World War II occurs:
(a) a day before midnight
(b) an hour before midnight
(c) less than a tenth of a second before midnight
(d) a hundredth of a second before midnight

8 John McNulty estimated that the global telecommunications network of 1975 was no more complex than a region of the brain less than the size of a ....

9 Peter Russell believes that crises may be an evolutionary catalyst in the push towards higher order. True/False

10 The product that photosynthesis produced, and which spelt death to the creatures of the time, was:
(a) carbon dioxide
(b) oxygen
(c) water
(d) sunlight

11 What would have been banned as 'selfish, unnatural and irres ponsible' if the creatures of the day when it evolved had had their say? ....

12 In the Chinese expression *wei-chi*, the first part of the word means:
(a) opportunity for change
(b) good luck
(c) beware of danger
(d) happy life

13 In the Chinese expression *wei-chi*, the second part of the word means:
(a) opportunity for change
(b) good luck
(c) beware of danger
(d) happy life

14 Russell believes that humanity can change its own destiny and actively shape the future. True/False

15 The evolutionary future of planet Earth lies within:
(a) the laps of the gods
(b) our own hands
(c) our own brains and minds
(d) the chaos theory

Check your answers against those on page 185.
Then divide your score by 15 and multiply by 100 to
calculate your percentage comprehension.

Comprehension score: .... out of 15
.... per cent

Now enter your score on your Progress Chart and your Progress Graph on page 187.

SUMMARY

1 The Mind Map Organic Study Technique incorporates all the major elements from previous approaches, as well as the state-of-the-art information on your brain, Mind Mapping and meta-guiding.

2 Begin with preparation (browse, set time to be spent and amount to be covered, do a previous knowledge Mind Map, establish goals). Then move on to application (Overview, Preview, Inview and Review).

HIGH EYE-CUE ACTION POINTS

1 Select an introductory, easy text on a topic you have always wanted to learn about but have somehow never got around to studying. Apply the Mind Map Organic Study Technique and all your advanced speed reading skills to complete the book in less than an hour. Mind Map the result.

2 Organize a five-minute-per-day practice session for accelerating your reading speeds with your guide.

ONWORD

How often have you felt oppressed and disheartened by the amount of information in the newspapers, magazines and other papers that pile up on your desk or shelves? The following chapter shows you how to deal with this situation with success and delight.

CHAPTER TWENTY

Getting Control of Your Newspapers, Magazines and Computer Screens

Newspapers, magazines and computer screens are some of your windows on the world and, increasingly, the universe. It is possible, by understanding their nature, and some new approaches to them, to increase your efficiency in this arena by a factor of ten.

FOREWORD
This chapter provides you with highly efficient new ways to extract relevant information from **newspapers**, **magazines** and **computer screens** which, together, make up more than 50 per cent of most people's reading (in some cases 100 per cent).

NEWSPAPERS
Newspapers are so much a part of our everyday life that we seldom stop to think that they are a very recent development. Before the twentieth century, the voice of journalism was virtually non-existent as far as the masses were concerned. Newspapers were, in the main, news-sheets containing very little analysis or editorial comment. There was, however, one noteworthy exception, *The Times*, whose critical reports on the Crimean War in 1855 have been cited as influential in the downfall of the Cabinet and the reorganization of the British Army.

The nineteenth century saw a steady growth in the world press, stimulated by the introduction of the Foudrinier machine which produced paper in a continuous sheet. Parallel to this development was the universal growth of communication networks and education: more information was required more rapidly, and more people were able to read. As a result, many of the world's newspapers were founded between 1840 and 1900

In the early twentieth century, newspapers flourished, but even now, after a fairly short existence, many are entering more difficult times. Reasons cited include the rise of television with its 'moving image' coverage of news events, and the spread of the computer news bulletin and the Internet which give more immediate and personal coverage of news events. Newspapers are currently fighting back, integrating themselves with these networks.

In the West we may well be entering a time in which the newspaper will change its function, dealing less with immediate news and more with summaries, analyses and comment.

It is worth taking a quick look around the world at the circulation and influence of other newspapers.

1 *Asahi Shimbun* of Tokyo. Circulation 9,000,000 copies per day. This paper is not simply a popular daily; it exerts enormous social and political influence.

2 *Jen Minh Jih Pao* of Peking. Circulation 2,500,000 copies per day. Although its circulation is not that high, this newspaper probably reaches more people than any other journal in the world. It is the channel of state information for the whole of China, and is read out over the radio, on trains, and in factories and on farms. Copies are also placed in glass-fronted cases, at intersections and market places.

3 *The New York Times*. Circulation 1,000,000 copies per day. Once again, the circulation figure here is misleading, for this newspaper is mainly read by leading economic, political and communication professionals in America and much of the western world. Its influence on international opinion-formers is therefore enormous.

As a matter of fact, the vast majority of the world's quality press seldom exceeds a daily circulation of 500,000 copies, and this includes three of the world's most educative and analytical newspapers: *Neue Zurcher Zeitung* of Switzerland, *The Times* of England and *Le Monde* of France. As with *Jih Pao* and *The New York Times*, the numerical circulation figures can be somewhat misleading in these cases, for the influence wielded by these newspapers is considerable.

Approaches to Reading Newspapers
Having viewed newspapers in their international and historical context, let us briefly discuss how best to read them.

1 First, it is most important to have an organized approach. Many people spend hours reading a newspaper and come away feeling no more enlightened than when they began.

2 Whatever newspaper you read, it is always helpful to decide beforehand exactly what your aim is. To assist you in this decision, always rapidly preview the newspaper before you read it, selecting the various passages and articles that you wish to read more thoroughly.

3 Also, make a note of the layout and typography. Knowing where articles are continued, for instance, saves a lot of page-turning and fumbling.

4 Most people have a tendency to buy a newspaper which supports their general views – in other words they give themselves a little pat on the back every morning or evening! It can be a most interesting exercise to buy a different newspaper each day for a week, comparing and contrasting the different layouts, the political bias, the approach of the reporters, the interpretation of news events, and the extent of the coverage. Try this during the coming week.

5 Newspaper reports should be checked for accuracy – I am sure that those of you who have been involved in a function or event which was reported the next day have often thought 'that's *nothing* like what happened at all!'.

News is written by people who are likely to be biased or to be following a particular editorial 'policy'. This 'misreporting', if we can call it that, is not necessarily intentional. Each person tends to see any given situation in a different light.

Newspaper reporters are individuals, and they may even be seeing a given event from a different physical location. (Being in the middle of a stampeding crowd and being in a building watching that crowd stampede, for example, are bound to produce different reports.)

6 Accepting this basic and inevitable bias, we move on to the reporting of the event itself. The journalist will take down brief notes of what he wishes to report, will spend time travelling back to his computer, and will then reconstruct in his mind's eye the events that have taken place. Once again, there will be slight and inevitable changes in emphasis which will be embellished by the words used to describe the situation.

Once the report has been written, it has to be edited, and then re-edited, before finally reaching the pages of the newspaper.

It can be seen that, even with the most sincere of intentions, it is almost impossible to give a completely objective report. Newspapers, magazines and journals should therefore be read with a far more critical eye than they usually are, and what they report should be checked against other sources such as radio, television, other journals and computer networks.

7 Having assimilated steps 1 to 6, you can now take your reading of newspapers a giant leap forward by following these guidelines:
(a) Decide on your main goals in reading a newspaper, and endeavour to stick to these goals as closely as possible.
(b) Skim and scan articles and pages using the techniques outlined in Chapter 9
(c) Use a guide throughout.
(d) As you skim and scan, mark any articles that are of particular interest.

(e) Cut out any articles that are going to be of lasting use and interest to you.

(f) Throw the rest of the newspaper out as soon as possible!

(g) Use a Mind Map to record any major new information or any information which is building on a daily or weekly or annual basis.

MAGAZINES

Magazines are like newspapers in most respects, and so the approaches outlined so far in this chapter will also apply to them. However, there are a number of significant differences which are worth noting.

• The articles in magazines tend to be longer than the articles in newspapers.

• Magazines tend to have more illustrations and more colour in those illustrations.

• Magazines are not produced within such a tight schedule, and therefore tend to be more discursive.

Because of these differences, it is usually easier to pick out a logical structure in a magazine article. Indeed, most magazine journalists are taught they should 'tell your reader what you're going to tell 'm, tell 'm, and then tell 'm you've told 'm.'

This means that most magazine articles start with a 'teaser' or 'grabber', immediately followed by a cogent statement of the purpose of the article. All this is the 'tell 'm what you're going to tell 'm'.

Next will follow the main body and bulk of the article. In a good article this will include logical arguments, illustrations, photographs and other elements drawing on the cortical skills to help persuade you of the writer's point. This is the 'tell 'm'.

The final part of the article, its climax, is where the writer uses some sort of dramatic or 'punchy' ending, incorporating a review of the main thesis, in an attempt to ram home the point. This is the 'tell 'm you told 'm'.

You will notice how close this formula is, as it should be, to the 'recall during learning curve' on page 156 (see also *Use Your Head* and *Use Your Memory*).

Knowing this structure will allow you to scan all magazine articles far more effectively, for you will know precisely where to look for the information. Skimming will also be much easier when you do it with this article structure uppermost in your mind.

Having a Magazine Blitz

One wonderful and enjoyable way of getting through your magazines, is to have a monthly 'magazine blitz'.

This means saving all your magazines for one special monthly occasion, in which you prepare yourself for a super meta-guide speed through every page of every magazine you have collected.

It is useful to set your metronome to at least 60 beats per minute, and to force yourself to turn the page with every beat, whipping your meta-guide down the page. The purpose of this exercise is for you to select only those pages from the magazine that you feel may be of interest to you. You should immediately rip these pages out and continue progressing through the magazine at your metronome pace. The pages you select should obviously include articles of particular interest. They can also include photographs or images that are particularly appealing, cartoons you especially like, advertisements that will be of use, etc. These you keep in a neat pile, discarding with a flourish the irrelevant material.

In the Buzan Centre Advanced Reading Courses, a fascinating statistic has emerged: in over 99 per cent of cases, the average amount of material retained after this first reading is between 2 per cent and 10 per cent. Some students felt so relieved by their sudden release from the massive weight of unread-material-that-had-to-be-completed that they whooped and hollered gleefully as they flung their discarded magazines into the centre of the class-room!

Once you have selected the relevant material, do a second read-through, this time sorting and collating them into appropriate categories. Because of the similarity of magazines aimed at the same readership, you will often find that a number of articles cover similar points, and your reading volume is thus reduced even further. Particularly beautiful images or witty cartoons can either be interspersed in other reading material to give you delightful breaks as you study, or can be filed in their own special sections.

Employing this approach usually results in less than one per cent of the magazine actually needing to be read – saving the other 99 per cent of effort!

Once you have completed your magazine blitz, any remaining material which you wish to save can be integrated into your knowledge file – see Chapter 21

COMPUTER SCREENS
Reading from computer screens can be made far easier by adjusting two main variables: the environment (especially lighting), and your reading technique.

Improving your Computer Environment

1 *Lighting:* Experiment with different kinds of lighting. You need an even, clear, soft light, with no glare. Inappropriate lighting can reduce your reading speed by as much as 50 per cent, so make sure that yours is appropriate for your needs.

2 *Contrast:* High contrast makes reading easier, and therefore comprehension better and speed faster. Different people prefer different colour combinations for print and background, so, once again, experiment to find the one most suitable for you. Common favourites include black print on a white background, orange on black, and navy-blue on white. Whatever your preference, adjust the contrast and brightness of your screen until you achieve the greatest possible print clarity. If the light in your office varies, vary your screen contrast to compensate.

Using Speed Reading Techniques on Your Computer Screen

1 *Use a meta-guide:* A long thin meta-guide, especially a chopstick or knitting needle, is particularly useful when reading from a computer screen. It allows you to read more comfortably and at a greater distance from the screen. The technique is identical to reading from the page of a book.

You can use the meta-guide in conjunction with the computer line pacer. Press the 'down' arrow, setting it at an appropriate speed, and let the guide cruise back and forward as the pages reveal themselves before you. If your posture and poise are appropriate, you will be more relaxed and at ease than the person who does not use a meta-guide.

Using this technique will get rid of the eye strain so commonly experienced by computer readers, as well as helping eliminate stiff necks, restricted breathing, hunched shoulders and lower back pain.

Make sure that every 10 or 15 minutes of computer speed reading is punctuated by a visual rest in which you allow your eyes to wander around the room and, ideally, into the medium and long distance. In this way you will eliminate the standard eye fatigue.

2 *Choose the right typeface:* The modern computer has a number of typefaces. Don't get stuck on a 'standard' one. Select the typeface that, at the time, feels easiest for your eye/brain system to assimilate.

3 *Choose the right line spacing:* Your computer has a variety of line-space settings. Choose the one that suits you best. Most popular is single-spaced setting, for this allows your peripheral vision a greater opportunity to take in large chunks of information per fixation.

Executive secretaries on a recent Management Centre Europe course for assistants to the directors of multinational organizations reported that 20–60 per cent of their day was spent reading informa-tion directly from computer screens, or from print-outs. They said that, with the increase in the amount of material faxed and emailed, these percentages were steadily increasing. The need for speed reading is thus even greater in the modern office.

The computer speed reading approaches outlined above will at least triple your speed on the computer screen. This means that the number of hours you will need to spend in front of the screen will be considerably reduced, thus further easing the strain on your eyes.

SUMMARY
Newspaper, magazine and computer-screen reading can become enjoyable, fun, quick and productive when you know and apply the appropriate speed reading techniques.

HIGH EYE-CUE ACTION POINTS
1 Subscribe to one or two newspapers for the next month, ideally selecting one which is different from what you have read before. For that month, apply *all* the techniques outlined on pages 165 to 167.
2 Do a magazine blitz on the pile of magazines you have been waiting to read for months (or even years!). If you are not in that common situation, select some appealing magazines during the coming weeks and do a magazine blitz on them.
3 Practise the computer speed reading approach on any screen with which you have contact during the next few days.

ONWORD
With your increasing facility at speed reading and assimilating infor-mation, and your new-found ability to select and order information from newspapers, magazines and computers, it is essential that you develop a 'super-system' for keeping your growing knowledge in your own personal library. The next chapter shows you the best way in which to do this.

CHAPTER TWENTY-ONE

Creating Your Knowledge File – Your Brain's External Data Bank

Knowledge is one thing; organized knowledge is a billion things!

FOREWORD

At this stage of *The Speed Reading Book*, you are ready to **create your own Knowledge File** – a 'data garden' which you can tend using the skills you have learnt.

CREATING YOUR KNOWLEDGE FILE

To create your Knowledge File, you need a standard loose-leaf ring binder, ideally large enough to take 500 pages. Within this, there should be dividers for each of your major areas of interest. You can discover these easily by doing a Mind Map, the centre of which is an image of yourself with an enquiring mind. Quickly Mind Map all those areas of knowledge that are of major interest to you, and the main branches of your Mind Map will provide an adequate first definition of your particular areas of interest.

KEEPING YOUR KNOWLEDGE FILE

Having defined your major areas of interest, the next stage is to save up information in each section. This you do by filing any summary Mind Maps you might have made during your reading and study in each of the areas, and especially by storing the articles you have selected when reading your newspapers and magazines (see Chapter 20).

TENDING YOUR KNOWLEDGE FILE

It is important to manage your time, your Knowledge File and yourself elegantly and effectively. One way to do this is to select appropriate articles and information over a period of a month in one given interest area, and to consider that information as a book or booklet. At the end of a month, read it as a book. Combine your speed reading skills with the Mind Map Organic Study Technique (see Chapter 19) and your reading effectiveness will be increased in a number of ways. Firstly, you'll have a similarly directed mental set while reading *every* article and piece of information; secondly, you will be obtaining the gestalt (whole picture) of all the information taken together; and thirdly, many 'different' articles published around the same time tend to repeat similar information – you can therefore save yourself an enormous amount of effort by skimming over repetitive areas.

MIND MAPPING YOUR KNOWLEDGE FILE
As you read your Knowledge File in these ways, keep growing on-going Mind Map summaries of your expanding knowledge. This constant process of review and integration will guarantee you not only greater understanding of the material, but also a much more accurate memory of it. This combination will lead you to the next stage: the Master Mind Map.

On your Master Mind Map you summarize all the major elements of any given area of knowledge. This is the 'Master Code' by which your brain can access its huge data banks. As your Master Mind Map grows, its boundaries will begin to link with those of other subjects, and what you already know will increasingly become an associational aid to knowing even more. The different areas of interest will begin to interlock more intricately, and you will eventually reach the stage of having truly comprehensive general knowledge. As this happens, you will realize that the more you know, the easier it is to know more!

AMAZING SHRINKING KNOWLEDGE FILES?!
Myself and those of my students who have developed Knowledge Files and Master Mind Maps have found an extraordinary event occurring after two to five years – our Knowledge Files have actually begun to shrink.

This is because, as your base of knowledge grows, so does your ability to remember and integrate additional knowledge.

As you continue to nurture your Knowledge File, you find that many articles you once thought 'important' can be discarded. Your Knowledge File thus becomes a condensed, elegant and timeless summary of the essences of your particular interests. You will have become a Master Learner.

HIGH EYE-CUE ACTION POINTS
1 Create, build and use your Knowledge File.
2 Practise your advanced meta-guiding techniques, preparing for your final Self Test and full acceleration.
3 Review the whole of *The Speed Reading Book* using your meta-guide, in readiness for your final Mind Map.

ONWORD
To the last two chapters and your final Self Test!

CHAPTER TWENTY-TWO

Getting Full Value from Literature and Poetry

Why Read Poetry and Literature? Because the great minds of history have left us, in them, easy stepping stones into the worlds of imagination, fantasy, ideas, philosophy, laughter and adventure; because by reading them you add to your own knowledge and your own historical and cultural data banks; because they are food for your soul.

FOREWORD

Literature is among the greatest expressions of human creativity. In this chapter you will be given the basic tools to appreciate it in the true sense of the word.

A novel is a massive conceptual achievement, and to appreciate it fully you need to be aware of the following aspects: **plot, theme, philosophy, standpoint, character development, mood and atmosphere**, **setting, imagery, symbolism** and **use of language**. Likewise, to appreciate **poetry** you should be aware of the different levels of meaning within any poem.

The more you understand each of these elements, the more your reading speed and comprehension will increase. If you are studying literature at school or university, the following aspects are invaluable as guide-posts for analysis. These guide-post areas will provide ideal main branches for your Mind Map notes, and good headings in essays and examinations.

INTRODUCTION

Many people proclaim that you cannot speed read a novel, because if you do you will lose the meaning and miss the rhythm of the language.

Nothing could be further from the truth.

A novel can be likened to an ocean. The little waves we see lapping the shore are in fact carried on waves which are nine ordinary waves long. These waves are themselves carried by waves which carry nine of them and these larger waves are similarly carried by waves which carry nine of *them*. Some waves in the ocean are miles long.

It is similar with a novel. The rhythms of language can be likened to the surface waves. The other, larger rhythms are the other, deeper elements of the novel. The speed reader can appreciate them all.

THE SPEED READING BOOK

THE ELEMENTS OF LITERATURE

Plot

Plot is the basic structure of events in a novel; the storyline, if you wish. It may play a relatively minor role in primarily descriptive writing or a major role in the better whodunnits and mystery novels.

Theme

The theme is what the plot is about. For example, in *The Forsyte Saga,* a series of novels which dealt with the history of a Victorian family, the main theme might variously be considered to be capitalism versus creativity, conservatism versus liberalism, conformity versus individuality, or wealth versus poverty. Sub-themes, which run parallel to the main one, frequently occur in novels. Sub-themes often concern minor love affairs and secondary characters.

Philosophy

Philosophy is the system of ideas governing the universe of the work, and can often be thought of as the author's commentary on the themes with which the book deals. Novelists known for the philosophical content in their novels include Dostoevsky, Dickens, Sartre and Thomas Mann.

Standpoint

Standpoint is *not* necessarily only the author's point of view or personal feeling about what he is writing. It is more often the physical standpoint from which the events described are seen. The author may, for instance, be all-knowing, standing apart, and viewing the past, present and future of the event he is describing (Henry James advocated abandoning this device as he felt it clouded true representation).

In contrast to this omniscient point of view, the author may place himself in the first person (the author becomes the 'I' of the book), as in Hammond Innes' adventure stories and *Lolita* by Nabokov.

Character Development

Character development concerns the changes the people in the story undergo. It may range from one extreme like Ian Fleming's James Bond who remains completely unchanged throughout his series of novels, to Etienne in Zola's *Germinal* who starts as a rebellious youth and evolves into a mature and dedicated man. Character development can also refer to the way the author presents the character, by description of their physical or mental character, movement, etc.

Mood and Atmosphere

These two terms refer to the manner in which the author evokes a sense of reality or unreality and the emotional response of the reader. Some people prefer to use only one of these terms, although they can be distinguished from each other: mood can be described as the reaction felt by the individual to the atmosphere of a piece of writing. For example, the atmosphere in Edgar Allen Poe's stories might be described as morbid and menacing, while the mood of his readers might vary from frightened to exhilarated.

Setting
Setting refers to the physical locale and the time period in which the events take place. Because the setting is usually quite apparent, its importance is often underestimated – yet the slightest variations in time and place often have very significant effects on plot, mood, atmosphere and imagery.

Imagery
Imagery is often described as the use of simile and metaphor, meaning that objects, people and events are described in creative or fanciful language. The root word 'image' is perhaps most useful in coming to an understanding of this term. For example, Sir Walter Scott, in *The Heart of Midlothian*, described Edinburgh as 'the pulsating heart core of the Scottish scene'; and Dickens, in *A Tale of Two Cities*, when describing the uncovering of a prisoner buried alive for 18 years, uses images of death and burial – heavy wreaths, cadaverous colours and emaciated heads and figures. Darkness and shadows prevail.

Symbolism
Simply explained, symbolism means that one thing stands for or represents another. Throughout much of literary history, the Earth, for example, has symbolized fertility and reproduction.

Since the publication of Freud's theories, symbolism has become an increasingly important element in literature, with a new emphasis on the sexual. Any jutting object, such as a gun or tree, may be used to symbolize the male sex organs; and any circular or hollow object, such as a box or a circular pond, can be used to symbolize the female sex organs. An excellent example of symbolism can be found in *A Tale of Two Cities*, when a cask of red wine is spilt. The populace drink the muddy dregs with relish, signifying the desperate hunger which later results in the spilling of real blood in the French Revolution. In D. H. Lawrence's *The Fox*, the frozen waste in which two women live symbolizes their frigidity, while the male character's shooting of a fox (symbolizing the general male 'threat') places him in the dominant male role.

Symbolism is often a great deal more obscure than in these examples, and the reader who understands it may be one of the very few who grasps the full meaning of much of great literature.

Use of Language
Authors' use of language varies from the tough masculine style of Hemingway to the flowing and poetic prose of Nabokov. The language an author uses is always revealing, and if you pay careful attention to it you will often gain far deeper insight into the shades of meaning and mood within the work.

In discussing these aspects of the novel I have dealt with each item separately, but it is important to remember they are all inextricably linked. The very setting of a story, for example, may be symbolic – and so it is with the other aspects. When you read literature, always try to be aware of the intricate interrelationships between all these aspects.

Poetry
Many people insist that poetry should be read very slowly. Our talking speed is about 200 words a minute, but many of us tend to read poetry at less than 100 wpm. Actually this hinders a proper appreciation, for a slow, plodding trudge through a poem effectively destroys the natural rhythm, and consequently conceals much of the meaning from the reader. In schools this problem is made worse by teachers who fail to correct students when they read each line as though the meaning lay at the end. This is often simply not the case. Sophisticated poets let their meaning flow *through* the lines.

The best approach to reading poetry is as follows:

1 Begin with a very rapid preview, enabling you to find out roughly what the poem is about and where it leads.
2 Then do a rapid but more thorough reading to get a more accurate idea of the way the lines relate to each other and the way the thought and rhythm interlink and progress.
3 Now take a leisurely ramble through the poem, concentrating on areas of particular interest.
4 Read the poem aloud.

In the final analysis speed is often irrelevant when it comes to literature and poetry – which can best be likened to listening to music or appreciating art. One does not listen to Beethoven's Fifth Symphony once and throw out the recording with the triumphant claim, 'Well, I've done that at an average speed of 33rpm!'

When reading literature and poetry, bring to bear on it all your knowledge and personal judgement, and if you feel it is the kind of writing you wish to treasure forever, forget about speeding through it and reserve it for those occasions when time is not so pressing.

SUMMARY
1 The novel can be compared to an ocean – it has many levels of meaning and each can be approached in a different way and at a different reading speed.

2 All its elements are interlinked.
3 Poetry, like the novel, should be read in levels, and initially much faster than most people would think appropriate.

HIGH EYE-CUE ACTION POINTS
1 Buy or borrow a book of poems, and read in the way described.

Your approach should be to apply whatever seems most appropriate from all that you have learnt. You should now begin to make your own decisions about the way you will tackle *any* given material.

When making these decisions, there are certain things that should remain constant, including your use of a guide, your focus on the goals for the reading, and your continuing ability to accelerate your reading speed while maintaining and improving your comprehension.

2 Choose a novel by one of your favourite authors and read it, using all the speed reading skills you have acquired so far. Make sure you preview it, Mind Map it, use your guide throughout, and analyse it according to the elements of the novel.

3 Read the following poems by the author, using the formula outlined opposite. A clue to the first one is that it relates very strongly to the information in Chapter 4. A clue to the second is that it relates to the ongoing theme of speed reading: the eye/brain perceptual system. The author would appreciate your interpretations and comments.

Dumbfounded

A Picture is Worth a Thousand Words.

I am led to understand that my three hundred million retinal light
   receivers absorb
one thousand two hundred million photons
each
one five-hundredth of a second

Five hundred
reality
snapshots of You,
every second

As I gaze,
amazed,

and you ask
somewhere in the far distance:

'What do you think?'

'Why don't you talk to me?'

Cliff and Man

The cliff-edge beckoned
asked him to walk near,
him to stand on edge;

but he tricked Her,
approached on cat feet
and buckled
his own length away –
slid his body forward;
safely moved his Seeing
over.

And she, laughing, made him swim,
stretched him in Her space,
dragged his mind's laceworks
down to the rock-mossed edges of depth,
reeled him down Her sides and ledges,
yo yo'd his Eye
and down and distantly
roared at him with Her sea.

He wrestled with her offering,
warped his tiny space;
engulfed Her.

So she flung him Her earth-bird
sea gull
who wrung his mind
to ecstasy,
rode the funnel
of Her deepness
feathered the winds that shoved him
still on that cliff edge
swept any curve
stilled any wind-rush
dropped in any air rise
erased ledge and edgeness for him
drew him   drew him out

The engulfer Engulfed.

ONWORD

One chapter to go! Now you have learnt how speed reading can help
you to appreciate literature and poetry fully, your last remaining
challenge in *The Speed Reading Book* is the final Self Test.

CHAPTER TWENTY-THREE

What You have Accomplished So Far – Your Extraordinary Possibilities for the Future

Create yourself. You create the future.

Your reading course is now nearing the end of its first stage. This stage is the completion of this book. The next stages will include your subsequent reviews of the book, your continuing practice of the new skills you have discovered, and your compilation of Mind Maps of all the books you read from now on which you wish to remember.

At this point it would be useful for you quickly to review the entire book, and to Mind Map the main points. You can use the Mind Maps in Plates I, IV, V, VI, VII and VIII to assist you with this.

Your continuing success in all fields of speed reading depends on your personal decision to continue the course you have begun, and on the capacity of your brain to read, assimilate, comprehend, recall, communicate and create – a capacity which we know approaches the infinite!

Your success is therefore guaranteed.

Your final Self Test will give you further information on your amazing brain. While reading it, bring to bear *all* the relevant knowledge you have gained from *The Speed Reading Book,* and do everything you can to surpass your previous performances. As you read 'Your Brain – The Enchanted Loom', you will realize that you are even more amazing than the amazing you have now begun to think you are.

Bon Voyage!

SELF TEST 7   Your Brain – The Enchanted Loom

The Human Brain and its Potential

The human brain is an enchanted loom where millions of flashing shuttles weave a dissolving pattern, always a meaningful pattern, though never an abiding one. It is as if the Milky Way entered upon some cosmic dance.

Sir Charles Sherrington

To compare the brain with a galaxy is in fact a modest analogy. Every intact person on our planet carries around his three-and-a-half-pound mass of tissue without giving much thought to it; yet every normal brain is capable of making more patterned interconnections than there are atoms in the universe.

The brain is composed of about ten billion nerve cells and each one is capable of being involved in a vast series of complex connections thousands of times every second. At a mathematical level alone, the complexity is astounding. There are ten billion neurons in the brain and each one has a potential of connections of 10^{28} In more comprehensible terms, this means that, if the theoretical number of potential connections in your brain were to be written out, you would get a figure beginning with 1, followed by about ten and a half million kilometres of noughts.

All this is potential, of course, and, despite the manifold detailed discoveries of neuro-physiology, it is your brain's potential which is most exciting. It is undisputed that we all under-use our brains – if we do not actually abuse them. This is hardly surprising. Few of us will ever see a human brain. Those who have, do not describe it as a particularly remarkable sight.

It is understandable that a concert pianist or a carpenter should value his hands above all, that a painter should cherish his eyes, that a runner should be most concerned about his legs. But hands are as useless without a brain as the piano itself without a player. The brain's potential has been largely underestimated precisely because of its omnipresence. It is involved in all we do, in everything that happens to us, and so we note that which is different in each experience, overlooking that without which nothing is possible for us.

We have been too much concerned with differences rather than potential in another, more important, sense. Since we have known that such things as brains existed, we have devoted most of our efforts not to improving them but to devising systems to demonstrate the differences between them. This applies not only in education, where pass or fail is the ultimate criterion, but in every aspect of our lives. We are American or Chinese, scholar or peasant, artist or scientist. These distinctions exist, of course, and it would be foolish to dismiss them completely. But the inherent ability of each brain in its own right is important too. In every head is a formidable powerhouse, a compact, efficient organ whose capacity seems to expand further towards infinity the more we learn of it.

John Rader Platt expressed this view:

If this property of complexity could somehow be transformed into visible brightness so that it would stand forth more clearly to our senses, the biological world would become a walking field of light compared to the physical world. The sun with its great eruptions would fade to a pale simplicity compared to a rose bush, an earthworm would be a beacon, a dog would be a city of light, and human beings would stand out like blazing suns of complexity, flashing bursts of meaning to each other through the dull night of the physical world between. We would hurt each other's eyes. Look at the haloed heads of your rare and complex companions. Is it not so?

The basis of this 'property of complexity' is the nerve cell – the neuron. Even those which are microscopically small are in themselves remarkably complex. Neurons differ from most other cells in that they are a more complicated shape and have many branching prolongations which can connect with each other to transmit nerve impulses. Throughout the nervous system the neurons vary tremendously in size. Some, running from the toes or the fingers into the spinal cord, can be as much as a metre in length. Others, in the cerebral cortex for example, are more than a thousand times smaller.

Everything we do, from moving a muscle to thinking great thoughts, involves intricate neuronal functioning. Whatever the activity, however, the process is similar and is founded on the excitation of the neuron. The process consists of electrochemical signals being passed from one neuron to another: not just singly or slowly but in rapid, multiple waves of communication. Each neuron has a main body which contains specific chemical and genetic information, and an axon which conducts the vital nerve impulses. It will also have a variable number of branching dendrites. These are the receivers of the impulses or information, either directly from a sense organ or, more commonly, from other neurons in the tapestry of connections.

The precise location of the transmission of the impulse from one neuron to another is your synapse where the information 'flows' across a microscopic gap not unlike the spark plug-gap or the distributor points in the internal combustion engine. The physics and chemistry of this process are immensely intricate. In the synapse chemical substances are released which enable the electrical impulses to be transmitted and the synapse has a threshold which affects how readily the impulse is accepted. In familiar or reflex activity the threshold is lower so that the circuit operates more readily. A higher threshold means that the signal is more difficult to transmit.

An impulse from a single neuron causes activation in the synapses it forms with others and even the simplest mental or physical process involves certainly hundreds of neurons receiving and transmitting impulses in complex cascading waves of communication and co-operation. A hundred thousand neuronal 'messages' a second is commonplace.

Everything we do and experience, therefore, involves this intricate bio-electrical process – from playing tennis to paying the bills. This is not as perplexing as it might seem. We know that the eyes do not in themselves see: they are merely lenses. The ears do not in themselves hear: they are, so to speak, microphones. When we watch a cricket match on television we do not see the players themselves but electronic representations of them on the picture tube. What is between the cat you see in the flesh and your brain's image of the cat is a series of neuro-physiological processes, just as there is a series of electronic processes between the actual cricket match and the image you see on television.

Our brains are, almost literally, everything. We can give more to them and in turn, and in addition, they can give to us. The brain is our secret, silent weapon. If we can just begin to use more of its power, we will indeed see a light that will hurt, but astonish, our eyes. To quote John Rader Platt again:

> Many of our most sensitive spirits today still see Man as the anti-hero; the helpless victim of weapons and wars, of governments and mechanisms and soul-destroying organizations and computers – as indeed he is. But in the midst of this man-made and inhuman entropy, like a Fourth Law of Man, there grows up even in the laboratories, a realization that Man is also mysterious and elusive, self-determining and perpetual. A lighthouse of complexity and the organizing child of the universe. One equipped and provided for to stand and choose and act and control and be.

* *

Stop Your Timer Now
Length of time: .... mins

Next, calculate your reading speed in words per minute (wpm) by simply dividing the number of words in the passage (in this case 1255) by the time (in minutes) you took.

Speed Reading Formula:
$$\text{words per minute (wpm)} = \frac{\text{number of words}}{\text{time}}$$

When you have completed your calculation, enter the number in the wpm slot at the end of this paragraph, and enter it on your Progress Chart and your Progress Graph on page 187.

Words per minute: ....

SELF TEST 7: COMPREHENSION
1 Who described the human brain as an enchanted loom?
(a) Sir Charles Sherrington
(b) Peter Russell

(c) John Rader Platt
(d) Isaac Newton

2 The human brain weighs approximately:
(a) 2 ½ lb
(b) 2 lb
(c) 3 ½ lb
(d) 3 lb

3 The number of potential connections for one brain cell is:
(a) 10^{10}
(b) 10^{19}
(c) 10^{28}
(d) 10^{39}

4 Since we have known that such things as brains existed, we have devoted most of our efforts:
(a) to improving them
(b) to devising systems to demonstrate the differences between them
(c) to dismissing them
(d) to destroying them

5 Who compared the complexity of the brain, transformed into visible brightness, with the physical world?
(a) Sir Charles Sherrington
(b) John Rader Platt
(c) Galileo
(d) Einstein

6 'The sun with its great eruptions would fade to a pale simplicity compared to a ....'

7 And 'a dog would be a':
(a) rose bush
(b) beacon
(c) sun
(d) city of light

8 The basis of the 'property of complexity of the brain' is the:
(a) nerve cell or neuron
(b) dendrite
(c) axon
(d) cortex

9 Neurons differ from most other cells in that they are:
(a) simpler
(b) more complicated in shape
(c) bigger
(d) smaller

10 Neurons can reach:
(a) a centimetre
(b) an inch
(c) a foot
(d) a metre

11 The process of electrochemical signals being passed from one neuron to another progresses:
(a) singly and slowly
(b) in rapid, multiple waves of communication
(c) faster than the speed of light
(d) only when we are thinking

12 An axon:
(a) is bigger than the brain cell
(b) is the main part of the synapse
(c) conducts vital nerve impulses
(d) is another name for the brain cell

13 The physics and chemistry of the processes in the synapse are fundamentally simple.   True/False

14 A common number of neuronal 'messages' per second is:
(a) 100
(b) 1000
(c) 10,000
(d) 100,000

15 Who wrote about the Fourth Law of Man?
(a) Einstein
(b) Freud
(c) Platt
(d) Sherrington

Check your answers against those on page 185.
Then divide your score by 15 and multiply by 100 to calculate your percentage comprehension.

Comprehension score:........ out of 15
.... per cent

Now enter your score on your Progress Chart and your Progress Graph on page 187.

Self Test Answers

SELF TEST 1 (Intelligence Wars)
1 False
2 (c) 40 per cent
3 (b) Dr Machado
4 True
5 (d) analysis with imagination
6 (a) place an image in the centre
7 (b) 1000 wpm
8 (b) Digital and Nabisco
9 (c) The Greeks
10 (a) a short rise
11 (c) 80 per cent
12 (c) a million million
13 False
14 (a) no evidence of brain cell loss with age in normal active and healthy brains
15 (d) 90

SELF TEST 2 (Art)
1 (b) Prehistoric times
2 (c) 40,000 to 10,000 BC
3 False
4 (c) religion
5 (d) bold outlines, flat colour
6 (b) yellow
7 (c) copies of Greek paintings found in the Roman cities of Pompeii and Herculaneum
8 (c) in the villas of wealthy Romans
9 True
10 (a) mosaic
11 True
12 (d) 1100
13 (b) avoided the realistic depiction of the human form
14 (c) Cezanne

SELF TEST 3 (Animal Intelligence)
1 (a) speak a number of different languages in a number of different dialects
2 False
3 (b) when communicating under water
4 (c) never attacked humans
5 (d) all the major oceans of the world
6 Pod

7 (c) within the range of human hearing
8 (c) 12
9 (b) passed from generation to generation
10 (d) centuries
11 False
12 (b) operates in a three-dimensional manner
13 (c) density
14 False
15 (c) see sound

SELF TEST 4 (Are We Alone?)
1 (b) 80
2 (c) the five hundreth anniversary of Columbus' discovery of America
3 False
4 (d) ten billion years ago
5 (a) Frank Drake
6 (c) Hercules
7 True
8 (c) six
9 (d) 304m (1000 feet) wide
10 (d) all the radio waves that hit it
11 (a) irregular and random
12 (c) he has been blind since birth
13 (b) Kent Cullers
14 False
15 Human

SELF TEST 5 (Baby Brain)
1 (b) has a full complement of cells before birth
2 (b) eight weeks after conception
3 (c) ten weeks before birth
4 (c) 25 per cent
5 (c) 50 per cent
6 (b) 75 per cent
7 (b) 90 per cent
8 True
9 (d) experiences a three-dimensional world immediately
10 The mother's voice
11 (c) faces
12 False

13 (d) had more connections between brain cells
14 (a) during 'brain spurts'
15 (c) the happiness and fulfilment of the child

SELF TEST 6 (The Awakening Earth)
1 (d) 15 billion
2 (b) February/March
3 (c) September
4 (b) October
5 (d) the last hour of the last day
6 (d) one and a half minutes before midnight
7 (c) less than a tenth of a second before midnight
8 Pea
9 True
10 (b) oxygen
11 Photosynthesis
12 (c) beware of danger
13 (a) opportunity for change
14 True
15 (c) our own brains and minds

SELF TEST 7 (Your Brain)
1 (a) Sir Charles Sherrington
2 (c) 3 ½ lb
3 (c) 1028
4 (b) to devising systems to demonstrate the differences between them
5 (b) John Rader Platt
6 Rose bush
7 (d) a city of light
8 (a) nerve cell or neuron
9 (b) more complicated in shape
10 (d) a metre
11 (b) in rapid, multiple waves of communication
12 (c) conducts vital nerve impulses
13 False
14 (d) 100,000
15 (c) Platt

VOCABULARY EXERCISE ANSWERS

Chapter 16
Exercise 1 (a)

1 l	2 e	3 m	4 f
5 n	6 g	7 o	8 d
9 k	10 c	11 j	12 b
13 i	14 a	15 h	

Exercise 1 (b)

1 e	2 i	3 d	4 n
5 j	6 f	7 k	8 c
9 a	10 l	11 g	12 o
13 m	14 h	15 b	

Exercise 1 (c)

1 h	2 a	3 o	4 b
5 k	6 c	7 n	8 d
9 l	10 m	11 g	12 j
13 f	14 i	15 e	

Chapter 17
Exercise 2 (a)

1 f	2 l	3 k	4 i
5 e	6 h	7 d	8 n
9 m	10 a	11 j	12 b
13 g	14 c	15 o	

Exercise 2 (b)

1 o	2 h	3 a	4 b
5 m	6 n	7 e	8 d
9 j	10 f	11 g	12 k
13 i	14 l	15 c	

Exercise 2 (c)

1 o	2 f	3 c	4 n
5 m	6 i	7 k	8 a
9 j	10 l	11 b	12 e
13 g	14 d	15 h	

Chapter 18
Exercise 3 (a)

1 h	2 d	3 b	4 l
5 e	6 n	7 a	8 j
9 m	10 o	11 g	12 i
13 c	14 k	15 f	

Exercise 3 (b)

1 d	2 a	3 k	4 h
5 j	6 l	7 n	8 m
9 o	10 b	11 g	12 f
13 c	14 e	15 i	

Exercise 3 (c)

1 e	2 k	3 d	4 l
5 a	6 o	7 i	8 n
9 m	10 j	11 g	12 b
13 c	14 f	15 h	

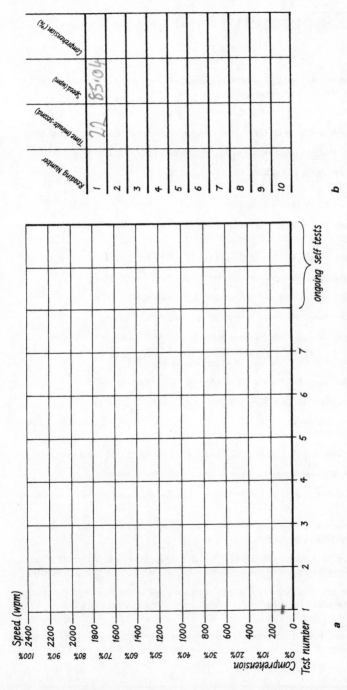

Fig. 16 *a* Progress graph *b* Progress chart. Ideally use one colour for your speed and another colour for your comprehension.

Bibliography

Atkinson, Richard C. and **Shiffrin, Richard M**. 'The Control of Short-term Memory.' *Scientific American*, August 1971

Baddeley, Alan D. *The Psychology of Memory*. New York: Harper & Row, 1976

Banton Smith, Ph.D., Nila. *Speed Reading Made Easier*. New York: Warner Books.

Berg, Howard Stephen. *Super Reading Secrets*. New York: Warner Books, 1992

Borges, Jorge L. *Fictions* (especially *Funes, the Memorious*). London: Weidenfeld & Nicolson, 1962

Brown, Mark. *Memory Matters*. Newton Abbot: David & Charles, 1977

Brown, R. and **McNeil, D**. 'The "Tip-of-the-Tongue" Phenomenon'. *Journal of Verbal Learning and Verbal Behaviour* 5, 325–37

Buzan, Tony. *Get Ahead*. IBC Publications, 1993 (with Vanda North).

Buzan, Tony. *Make the Most of Your Mind*. London: Pan, 1988

Buzan, Tony. *Use Your Head*. London: BBC Books, 1989

Buzan, Tony. *Use Your Memory*. London: BBC Books, 1989

Coman, Marcia J. and **Heavers, Kathy L**. *NTC Skill Builders: What You Need to Know About Reading Comprehension & Speed, Skimming & Scanning, Reading for Pleasure*. Illinois, USA: National Textbook Company, 1992

Cutler, Wade E. *Triple Your Reading Speed*. USA: Macmillan (Arco).

Ebbinghaus, H. *Uber das Gedachtnis*. Leipzig: Duncker, 1885 op.

Frank, Stanley D. *Remember Everything You Read: The Evelyn Wood 7-Day Speed Reading & Learning Program*. New York: Avon Books.

Fry, Ron. *How To Study Program: Improve Your Reading*. USA: Career Press.

Gelb, Michael. *Present Yourself*. London: Aurum Press, 1988

Haber, Ralph N. 'How We Remember What We See.' *Scientific American* **105**, May 1970

Howe, J. A. and **Godfrey, J**. *Student Note-Taking as an Aid to Learning*. Exeter: Exeter University Teaching Services, 1977 op.

Howe, M. J. A. 'Using Students' Notes to Examine the Role of the Individual Learner in Acquiring Meaningful Subject Matter.' *Journal of Educational Research* **64**, 61–3

Hunt, E. and **Love, T**. 'How Good Can Memory Be?' in *Coding Processes in Human Memory*, 237–60, edited by A. W. Melton and E. Martin. Washington DC: Winston/Wiley, 1972 op.

Hunter, I. M. L. 'An exceptional memory'. *British Journal of Psychology* 68, 155–64, 1977

Keves, Daniel. *The Minds of Billy Milligan*. New York: Random House, 1981; London: Bantam, 1982

King, Graham. *The Secrets of Speed Reading*. London: Mandarin, in association with the *Sunday Times*, 1993

Klaeser, Barbara Macknick. *Reading Improvement*. Chicago: Nelson Hall, 1977
Loftus, E. F. *Eyewitness Testimony*. Cambridge, Mass.: Harvard University Press, 1980

Luria, A. R. *The Mind of a Mnemonist*. Cambridge, Mass.: Harvard University Press, 1987

Maberley, Norman C. *Mastering Speed Reading*. New York: Penguin (Signet), 1978

Maddox, Harry. *How to Study*, New York: Fawcett Premier, 1988

Minninger, Ph.D., Joan. *Rapid Reading in 5 Days*. New York: Perigee Books (The Berkley Publishing Group), 1994

O'Brien, Dominic. *How to Pass Exams*. Headline Book Publishing, 1995

Penfield, W. and **Perot, P**. 'The Brain's Record of Auditory and Visual Experience: A Final Summary and Discussion.' *Brain* **86**, 595–702

Penfield, W. and **Roberts, L**. *Speech and Brain-Mechanisms*. Princeton, NJ: Princeton University Press, 1959 op.

Ruger, H.A. and **Bussenius, C. E**. *Memory*. New York: Teachers College Press,1913 op.

Russell, Peter. *The Brain Book*. London: Routledge & Kegan Paul, 1966; Ark, 1984

Schaffzin, Nicholas Reid. *The Princeton Review – Reading Smart*. New York: Villard Books.

Standing, Lionel. 'Learning 10,000 Pictures.' *Quarterly Journal of Experimental Psychology* **25**, 207–22

Stratton, George M. 'The Mnemonic Feat of the "Shass Pollak".' *Physiological Review* **24**, 244–7

Suzuki, S. *Nurtured by love: a new approach to education*. New York: Exposition Press, 1969

Thomas, E.J. 'The Variation of Memory with Time for Information Appearing During a Lecture.' *Studies in Adult Education*, 57–62, April 1972

Tulving, E. 'The Effects of Presentation and Recall of Materials in Free-Recall Learning.' *Journal of Verbal Learning and Verbal Behaviour* **6**, 175–84

von Restorff, H. 'Uber die Wirkung von Bereichsbildungen im Spurenfeld.' *Psychologische Forschung* **18**, 299–342

Wagner, D. 'Memories of Morocco: the influence of age, schooling and environment on memory.' *Cognitive Psychology* **10**, 1–28, 1978

Yates, F.A. *The Art of Memory*. London: Routledge & Kegan Paul, 1966; Ark, 1984

Zorn, Robert. *Speed Reading*, New York: Harper Perennial, 1991

Index

Page numbers in *italic* refer to
the illustrations

Adam, Sean, 31, 71
ageing, 21
Alexeyenko, Eugenia, 73–4
Asahi Shimbun, 165
assimilation, reading, 33
atmosphere, literature, 174–5
Attention Deficit Hyperactivity
Disorder (ADHD), 117–19
Attention Disability Disorder
Syndrome (ADDS), 117–19

back-skipping, 81–2, 113–14
brain:
  ageing, 21–2
  brain reading, 76–8
  cells, 21
  left and right cortex, 18
  occipital lobe, 37
  potential, 179–82
  reading posture, 55
  relativism, 103

chairs, 54
character development, literature,
  174
communication, reading, 34
comprehension, 16–26, *26*, 38–40,
  120–4
computer screens, 168–70
concentration, 121–4
conceptual difficulty, 121

daydreaming, 123
descriptive paragraphs, 130
desks, 54
double guide, *84*, 85
double line sweep, *80*, 81
dyslexia, 114–17, *114*

environment, *53*, 56–7

explanatory paragraphs, 130
extra-integration, reading, 33–4
eyes:
  guiding, 58–62, *60*, *61*
  ideal conditions for reading, 53–5
  movements, 36–40, *39*
  reading environment, *53*, 56–7
  scanning, 97–102
  visual field, 74–8, *76*, *77*

finger-pointing, 58, 113

guides, 58–62, *60*, *61*
  finger-pointing, 58, 113
  meta-guiding, 79–96, *80*, *83*, *84*,
    169

health problems, 57
horizontal vision, 74–8
hyperactivity, 117–19

imagery, literature, 175
information explosion, 27
interest, lack of, 122–3
intra-integration, reading, 33

Jefferson, Thomas, 120
Jen Minh Jih Pao, 165

Kennedy, John F., 31, 70, 75
key words, 126–7, *126*
Knowledge Files, 171–2

language, literature, 176
  see also vocabulary
lazy 'S', *84*, 85
learning:
  learning problems, 114–19
  memory loss after, 20–1
  study reading, 154–63, *155*, *156*
Lees, C. Lowell, 70
left cortex, 18
light, 53–4, *53*, 169

linking paragraphs, 130–1
literature, 173–8
look-say method, 28
loop technique, 82, *83*

magazines, 167–8
Magliabechi, Antonio di Marco, 71–3, 75
Master Code, 172
Master Mind Map, 172
memory:
  memory loss, 20–1
  mnemonic techniques, 20
  photographic memory, 79–96
mental abilities, ageing and, 21–2
mental set, 122
meta-guide, 79–96, *80, 83, 84*, 169
  techniques, 79–85
metronome training method, 103–5
Mill, John Stuart, 69, 75
Mind Map Organic Study Technique (MMOST), 154–63
Mind Maps, 18–19, 125, 127–8
mind's eye, 75–6
mnemonic techniques, 20
mood, literature, 174–5
motivation, lack of, 123

The New York Times, 165
newspapers, 164–7
North, Vanda, 31, 71
note-taking, 125–7, *126*
novels, 173–7

organization, 122

paragraph structure, 130–1
perception exercises, 40–5
peripheral vision, 74–8, *77*
philosophy, literature, 174
phonic method, 27–8
photographic memory, 79–96
plot, literature, 174
Plus One Rule, 46
poetry, 173, 176, 177–8
posture, *53*, 55
prefixes, 135–41
previewing, 132–3

range reading, 19
reading:
  goals, 120
  new definition, 33–5
  reading problems, 112–14
  reading speeds, 16–26, 121
  teaching children, 27–8
recall, 34, *155, 156*
recognition, reading, 33
record holders, speed reading, 31
regression, 113–14
relativistic brain, 103
retention, reading, 34
reverse sweep, *80*, 81–2
right cortex, 18
Roosevelt, Franklin D., 69–70
Roosevelt, Theodore, 97
roots, vocabulary, 147–51

'S' technique, 82, *83*
scanning, 97–102
screens, computer, 168–70
setting, literature, 175
skimming, 97, 98–102
speed reading, 28–32
  reading speeds, 16–26, 121
  record holders, 31
standpoint, literature, 174
study reading, 154–63, *155, 156*
sub-vocalization, 28, 112–13
suffixes, 142–6
super-speed reading, 19
symbolism, literature, 175

tachistoscopes, 28–9, *30*
theme, literature, 174

variable sweep, *80*, 81
vertical vision, 74–8
vertical wave, *84*, 85
vocabulary, 121, 134–5
  prefixes, 135–41
  roots, 147–51
  suffixes, 142–6

zig-zag technique, 82, *83*

BUZAN CENTRES
MAKE THE MOST OF YOUR MIND

The company for all brain-related courses, products and books.

The only organization licensed to deliver customized courses in Tony Buzan's Mind Map® methods.

TRAINING COURSES

A portfolio of programme formats are available, individually designed for our clients. We provide the training that will give you immediate performance results.

FOR:
• Companies • Education Authorities • Government Departments •
• Schools • Local Authorities • Individuals •

PLUS: in-depth 'TRAIN THE TRAINER' licensing courses

For a brochure please contact:

UK HEAD OFFICE Buzan Centres Ltd. 54 Parkstone Road, Poole, Dorset BH15 2PX
Tel: 44 (0) 1202 674676 *Fax:* 44 (0) 1202 674776
Email: 101737.1141@compuserve.com
USA OFFICE Buzan Centres Inc. 415 Federal Highway, Lake Park, Florida, 33403 USA
Tel: 1 (561) 881 0188 *Fax:* 1 (561) 845 3210 *Email:* Buzan000@aol.com

JOIN

THE BRAIN CLUB
54 Parkstone Road, Poole, Dorset BH15 2PX

The organization for anyone who has a brain and wants to learn how to use it.

As the brain-child of Tony Buzan, the Brain Club was launched in 1987 as a self-help organization for people of any age, to help improve the way we think, learn and study.

The company's aims and policies are:
to promote research into and the development of the capabilities of the human brain.

Please send for full information.